ISBN: 9781290461979

Published by:
HardPress Publishing
8345 NW 66TH ST #2561
MIAMI FL 33166-2626

Email: info@hardpress.net
Web: http://www.hardpress.net

BOOKS ON CLIMBING.

Climbs in the New Zealand Alps : Being an Account of Travel and Discovery. By E. A. FITZ GERALD, F.R.G.S., and with contributions by Sir MARTIN CONWAY, PROF. BONNEY, and C. L. BARROW. Illustrated by JOSEPH PENNELL, H. G. WILLINK, and A. D. MCCORMICK, and from photographs ; together with a New Map. Cloth, 31s. 6d. nett. Also an Edition de Luxe, on Japan paper, frontispiece portrait of the author, by Sir E. BURNE-JONES, price £5 5s. nett.

740 pages, cloth, price 31s. 6d. nett.

Climbing and Exploration in the Karakoram-Himalayas. By Sir WILLIAM M. CONWAY, M.A., F.S.A., F.R.G.S. 300 Illustrations by A. D. McCORMICK, and a Map.

Supplementary Volume of Scientific Memoranda, &c., to

Climbing and Exploration in the Karakoram-Himalayas. With Photogravure Portrait of Sir W. M. Conway, and his Maps, and Scientific Reports by Prof. T. G. Bonney., D.Sc, F.R.S., Dr. A. G. Butler, F.L.S., F.Z.S., Sir W. M. Conway, W. Laurance H. Duckworth, B.A., Lt.-Colonel A. G. Durand, C.B., W. Botting Hemsley, F.R.S., W. F. Kirby, F.L.S., F.E.S., Miss C. A. Raisin, B.Sc., Prof. C. F. Roy. With frontispiece portrait of the author, cloth, 15s. nett ; or, in binding uniform with the Edition de Luxe of the former volume, price 21s. nett.

Third Edition.

My Climbs in the Alps and Caucasus. By A. F. MUMMERY. Illustrated from Original Drawings and Photographs by JOSEPH PENNELL, A. HOLMES, J. WOOLEY, SELLA, and other artists. Super Royal 8vo, cloth, 21s. nett.

An Artist in the Himalayas. By A. D. McCORMICK. Illustrated with over 50 Original Sketches made on the Journey. Large Crown 8vo, cloth gilt, 16s.

In Preparation.

Climbing Reminiscences of the Dolomites, 1893. By LEONE SINIGAGLIA. Translated from the Italian by MARY ALICE VIALLS.

CONWAY & COOLIDGE CLIMBERS' GUIDES.

Edited by Sir WILLIAM M. CONWAY and Rev. W. A. B. COOLIDGE. 32mo, limp cloth, gilt lettered, with pocket, flap, and pencil, price 10s. each. Also, a Series of SIX COLOURED MAPS of the ALPS OF THE DAUPHINY, mounted on linen, and strongly bound in cloth case, price 4s. 6d. the set.

1. **The Central Pennine Alps.** By Sir WILLIAM MARTIN CONWAY.

2. **The Eastern Pennine Alps.** By Sir WILLIAM MARTIN CONWAY.

3. **The Lepontine Alps** (Simplon and Gothard). By Rev. W. A. B. COOLIDGE and Sir WILLIAM M. CONWAY,

4. **The Central Alps of the Dauphiny.** By Rev.W.A. B. COOLIDGE, H. DUHAMEL and F. PERRIN.

5. **The Chain of Mont Blanc.** By LOUIS KURZ.

6. **The Adula Alps of the Lepontine Range.** By Rev. W. A. B. COOLIDGE.

7. **The Mountains of Cogne.** By GEORGE YELD and W. A. B. COOLIDGE. With Map.

8. **The Range of the Todi.** By Rev. W. A. B. COOLIDGE.

9. **The Dolomites.** By N. NERUDA

LONDON : T. FISHER UNWIN.

THE KARAKORAMS AND KASHMIR

The Karakorams
and Kashmir

An Account
of a Journey

BY

OSCAR ECKENSTEIN

LONDON
T. FISHER UNWIN
1896

To

MY FRIEND

THE HEATHEN

THIS ACCOUNT OF MY EXPERIENCES IN

HIS COUNTRY IS DEDICATED.

PREFACE.

THIS small book is not a work upon Kashmir, but a description of the principal matters which struck me on a journey which I made there. It neither formulates general views as to that country, nor criticises those formulated by others. Consisting of letters written home at the time and of entries made in my diary, it records no more than the impressions made upon me personally by the sights and incidents which I saw. Those impressions were so vivid that I am almost encouraged to hope that, even if I have only transcribed a small part of them, some readers may nevertheless share the enjoyment which my journey gave me.

x *Preface.*

Neither my letters nor my diary were written for publication. I have, however, thought it best—for two reasons—to alter them as little as possible. I wish, on the one hand, to keep the narrative as it originally was—an unsophisticated statement of actual impressions as they occurred. On the other hand, I know that if the subject-matter does not give sufficient interest to the narrative, I have no literary experience or skill which can enhance it.

Some part of my journey is, I understand, referred to in Sir W. M. Conway's book, "Climbing and Exploration in the Karakoram Himalayas," and in Mr. McCormick's book, "An Artist in the Himalayas"; but I have thought that it would be more satisfactory to me to defer reading those books till this account has been independently published.

INTRODUCTION.

FOR more than twenty years my own work has been mainly scientific, and my play has been, whenever opportunity offered, the climbing of mountains. In the summer of 1891 I met Professor (now Sir) W. M. Conway at Zermatt, where we had often met before; and when he asked whether I was disposed to join him in an expedition to the Karakoram mountains to climb and to make geographical and other exact observations, I had no difficulty in realising that, if the trip were practicable, I should very much like it. My own engagements made it difficult for me to accept; but ultimately things were arranged, and I was able to agree that I would join. The expe-

xii   *Introduction.*

dition was to be assisted by the Royal Geographical Society, and was to consist of the Hon. C. G. Bruce (son of Lord Aberdare, a late President of the Royal Geographical Society), Professor Conway, and myself, accompanied by the Alpine guide, Mattia Zurbriggen, or Del Ponte, of Macugnaga. Later on it was also arranged that Mr. A. D. McCormick, an artist, should join the party.

The plan of the expedition was this: Starting from Srinagar, the expedition was to go *viâ* Skardu to Askole, and there in the first instance attempt the ascent of the peak. Mungo Gusor, the central position of which makes it particularly valuable as a point of view for topographical purposes. After this we were to ascend the Baltoro Glacier, attempting thence to ascend peaks, particularly K2, and to explore passes. We were then to pay a short visit to the Punmah Glacier, and thereafter attempt to reach the top of the R Zong La, the old pass formerly used as a route between Hunza and Nagyr and Skardu by native tribesmen. We were then to descend for some distance down the great Hispar Glacier, and then turn south and come over the Nushik La to Arandu.

If there was any time left, it was to be devoted to the exploration of the Chogo Lungma Glacier.

Generally we were to survey the mountains and glaciers, make such scientific observations as were practicable, and make collections of plants, minerals, etc. We wished in particular to reach as great an altitude as possible, in order to obtain information on the much discussed and as yet quite unsettled questions as to the physiological effect of reduced pressure of atmosphere on the human system.

A part of this programme was carried out. Of the remainder, some part could not have been under the circumstances in which we found ourselves. The condition, for instance, of some of our instruments was such that xiv *Introduction.*

they could not be used for reliable observations. I have no doubt, however, that on these points ample information will be found in Sir W. M. Conway's works ; and as they are only incidentally material to my present purpose, the reproduction of the impressions which I received on the journey, I need not further discuss them here.

CONTENTS.

CHAP.		PAGE
I.	SRINAGAR, SATURDAY, APRIL 2, 1892 .	1
II.	SRINAGAR, THURSDAY, APRIL 7 .	16
III.	BANDIPUR, THURSDAY, APRIL 14 .	26
IV.	BURZIL, WEDNESDAY, APRIL 20 .	31
V.	BURZIL, SUNDAY, APRIL 24 .	37
VI.	ASTOR, SATURDAY, APRIL 30 .	45
VII.	BUNJI, SATURDAY, MAY 7 .	55
VIII.	GILGIT, SATURDAY, MAY 14 .	68
IX.	DIRRAN, SATURDAY, MAY 21 .	79
X.	GILGIT, SUNDAY, MAY 29 .	90
XI.	GILGIT, TUESDAY, JUNE 7 .	98
XII.	NAGYR, THURSDAY, JUNE 16 .	118
XIII.	NAGYR, MONDAY, JUNE 27 .	137
XIV.	HAIGUTTUM, MONDAY, JULY 4 .	148

xvi

Contents.

CHAP.		PAGE
XV.	ARANDU, THURSDAY, JULY 7	161
XVI.	SKARDU, WEDNESDAY, JULY 13	179
XVII.	ASKOLE, TUESDAY, AUGUST 2	190
XVIII.	SKARDU, FRIDAY, AUGUST 12	202
XIX.	SRINAGAR, MONDAY, AUGUST 29	217
XX.	SRINAGAR—CONCLUSION	228
XXI.	APPENDIX—ROUTES	241

I.

Srinagar, Saturday, April 2, 1892.

WE left England in the February of 1892 and travelled in the usual way by steamer and rail to Hassan Abdal. Then we went by mail tonga (a sort of mail cart) to Abbotabad, the important military station, where we arrived on March 10th. So far all travelling arrangements were distinctly luxurious. At Abbotabad we lived in much comfort in Bruce's house (the height of which above sea level is about 4,240 feet by B. P. determination) and were treated with great, I almost might say excessive, hospitality by

2 *The Karakorams and Kashmir.*

the officers stationed there. May their shadow never grow less !

Abbotabad is a beautifully situated spot. It lies in a broadish valley, with mountains running up on each side some 4,000 feet to 5,000 feet. It consists of a number of houses, each with considerable grounds, and so covering a good space. There was still plenty of snow on the surrounding hills, for it was only just the end of winter ; and from a little hill called Brigade Circular, some 750 feet up, we could see in the far distance—perhaps one hundred miles, perhaps two hundred miles off—some mighty mountain masses running up to 20,000 feet or more, with glaciers plainly visible and recognisable as such.

It was at Abbotabad that I first encountered the heathen merchant, and became aware of his peculiar way of doing business. While I was writing my first letter home, I was enjoying a mixed conversation in broken English and Hindustani with a native mer-

Srinagar. 3

chant, who was trying to sell a piece of embroidery to me. The transaction took altogether two days. The first day he commenced by asking 75 rupees for it ; later on he was very anxious to toss whether I was to give him 40 or 50 rupees for it—verily it is a strange land. I had originally offered 10 rupees for it ; but later on I withdrew my offer, and proposed five. This seemed to grieve him, and he made most pathetic appeals to my better feelings. The bargaining proceeded through two-thirds of a long letter, of which it relieved the monotony, and it ultimately resulted in the transfer of the embroidery to me for 10 rupees. I thought it was worth it, and the native also seemed pleased.

We have been joined by an American friend of Conway's, Mr. J. H. Roudebush, a fine tall young man of about twenty, who is entirely without any experience of mountain-climbing. He is going to travel with us till a convenient shooting ground is reached,

4   *The Karakorams and Kashmir.*

and then he intends to amuse himself with shooting in company with another man, Colonel Lloyd-Dickin, who also is to accompany us so far.

We were delayed a few days at Abbotabad by our heavy luggage; Roudebush and Lloyd-Dickin left us to try and get some sport on the way here; but at last, on March 28th, the rest of us started.

We certainly formed a most imposing procession. First of all there was our heavy luggage which was loaded on twenty mules; then there were the mule-drivers, and three Ghurka soldiers, of whom Parbir (who had been in Zermatt last December with Bruce and myself) was the boss in charge; he being responsible for luggage, mules, &c., till he hands it over to us here. The other two are called Lilaram and Herkir. They all three belong to the Thapa clan. Of course the mules were bound to occupy much more time on the journey than we, as they did only one march a day; a "march" on this

Srinagar. 5

way apparently being anything between ten and sixteen miles. The mules, &c., were kindly placed at our disposal by the benevolent Indian Government; which Government, I may incidentally remark, appears to be the most sensible I have yet struck. We ourselves went in native vehicles called "ekkas." An "ekka" is emphatically an invention of the devil. It is a two-wheeled contrivance devoid of any kind of or apology for springs. It holds two people, one passenger and the driver; there is a cubical-shaped box, about 3 feet cube, in which the two people have to find room, the driver squeezing up in one corner in front, on the off side, and the passenger in the near back corner. The bottom of this box is about 5 feet off the ground; and as the wheels are about 4 feet 6 inches in diameter, stability is chiefly distinguished by its absence. What with jolting and the uncomfortable position one is screwed into, it is far and away the worst means of progression that I have ever

6 *The Karakorams and Kashmir.*

attempted, and I don't want more of it than I can possibly help. In this case, however, we had to put up with them ; and there were therefore added to the procession five ekkas, containing Conway, McCormick, Zurbriggen, myself, and last, but not least, the "bearer," Rahim Ali by name. The latter—who has so far been Bruce's head servant—comes with us as our universal factotum. He is a native, Mahometan, age over fifty, but looks about thirty to my eye. He is a very excellent cook, and understands a certain amount of English, particularly in the line of profanity, in which he uses new and weird combinations.

We started at 2.40 p.m., and drove by a good road to Mansera Dawk Bungalow (about seventeen miles) where we arrived at 5.20 p.m. and stopped for the night.

A "Dawk Bungalow" is, as far as I know, a purely Indian institution. At every convenient stage on a road a house is built by the Government for the accommodation of

Srinagar. 7

travellers. This is furnished with chairs, tables, &c., and the traveller can put up there for the night, cook his meals, &c., for which he has to pay a small charge, viz., 8 annas for using the bungalow for three hours or less, and 1 rupee for twenty-four hours. Some few things in the way of supplies can be obtained at fixed rates from the native who is in charge. Food is exceedingly cheap here ; a fowl is 6 to 8 annas ; a sheep is 4 to 6 rupees ; so that living costs very little. One rupee a head a day gives a man everything he may desire in the way of food, and the food is very good too.

At Mansera there is a curious old moraine, which Conway and I walked over and examined in the evening. I much regretted not having taken a shooting tool with me as a fine wild cat jumped up within a few feet of us, and would have been a certain bag if one had had even a revolver.

So far the road was, on the whole, fairly level, but very winding. From Mansera,

8 *The Karakorams and Kashmir.*

however (which we left by the same ekkas at 8.20 a.m. on 29-3-92), it went up to a pass (10.50 a.m.) through a dense forest chiefly of pine ; the appearance of the hills and scenery being very much like that of the Black Forest in Germany. The pass is on the watershed on the west side of Khagan. Then the road descends rapidly to Garihabibulla, a village on the Kishan Ganga river about 3,400 feet above sea level by aneroid. The Dawk Bungalow, where we lunched (reached at 1 p.m.), is on the right bank of the river, the village being on the left bank. There is a fine bridge across. Here we discharged our ekkas, and engaged ten coolies as porters, to carry our personal luggage, leaving the mules to come by another route.

We started with the coolies at 3 p.m. ; crossed the bridge and went down the left bank of the stream for a long way—a long, stony walk much reminding one of parts of the Saas valley. Then the path ascends the

Srinagar. 9

hills, and a small pass was reached at 5.55 p.m., height about 4,000 feet by aneroid. From the pass the path runs nearly level along the hillside for a longish distance, and then there is a steep descent down to Dhomel, which is situated at the junction of the Kishen Ganga and Jhelam rivers. We reached the Dawk Bungalow there at 7.20 p.m., after crossing both rivers by suspension bridges of curious construction, supposed to be due to the vagaries of an electrical engineer. At Dhomel there is a very excellent Dawk Bungalow, where we stopped for the night.

The next morning (Wednesday, 30–3–92) we engaged five ekkas; there was trouble before we got under way, and it took much profanity and a little violence. Finally we started off at 10 a.m. The ekkas were very rotten, and the drivers at first somewhat inclined to be troublesome; but that was soon stopped. From here the road winds up the valley, the river running below in

10 *The Karakorams and Kashmir.*

a nullah, of which the sides are in places certainly over 1,000 feet high.

A "nullah" or "nala" is a curious, and very characteristic feature of the country. It is simply a deep cutting in which there is, or has been, a river. The sides are either actually or approximately vertical; sometimes the width is many times the height, or *vice versâ*, or anywhere between. The greatest width I have seen at present is about one mile. The bottom of a nullah is approximately level, and they have a very curious look to the stranger.

We arrived at Chakoti Dawk Bungalow at 5.30 p.m., and stopped there for the night. We left at 6.45 a.m. the next morning (31–3 92) on the same ekkas. Three miles before Uri one ekka (with Zurbriggen) went off the road, rolled down over the embankment, and there was a general upset.

Zurbriggen was, luckily, not much damaged—only a few trifling scratches and bruises. The native driver escaped without

Srinagar. 11

damage at the time, but suffered subsequent damage from us. The upper part of the ekka was smashed to smithereens ; but the wheels and the lower part of the frame held together, and so we managed to patch it up. Zurbriggen changed over into my ekka, and I, for the rest of the journey, went in the damaged one (which was not more uncomfortable than the complete article, that's impossible), and made the driver's life a misery to him.

We reached Uri at 10 a.m., and had breakfast ; then on to Rampur (3 p.m.). Here we intended to lunch, but there was a difficulty in getting supplies. Our bearer, by a process of banging the native official about, induced him ultimately to procure some ; but as this had occupied some time we thought it best to drive on, and so we did, arriving at Baramulla at 6.45 p.m. Here the Jhelam is navigable, so we left our ekkas, and I was just thankful to get out of those wretched conveyances. Every joint of my body

12   *The Karakorams and Kashmir.*

seemed to have got out of adjustment. Here we took two boats, which were to be our home for some little while ; indeed, they are so at present.   These boats are very heavy, and of a perverse construction, for the bottom is curved lengthwise and flat crosswise.   They reminded me of the rocking-horse of my youth.

We had dinner on board, and then slept the sleep of the tired with great satisfaction. We started next morning (1–4–92) at 8.45 a.m.   The stream was very sluggish, and progress would have been very easy if it were not for the extraordinary build of our boats.   As it is progression was slow, chiefly by towing and occasional punting, and was attended with a vast waste of energy.   The native is peculiar ; he thinks that if he exerts his muscles considerably he is doing his best, and that with an utter disregard of how he applies his strength, and with curious Oriental perversity he of course applies it in almost the worst way possible.   Towards noon we

Srinagar. 13

began to enter the Walar lake; the shores all round are very low, and it is difficult to say how far the lake extends. We crossed a corner of the lake, and in the afternoon we entered a canal, a short way up which we stopped for the night. An early start was made on Saturday while we were still asleep. The canal soon narrowed exceedingly, and there was consequently a stronger current, particularly round the sides of our boats, as the canal was very shallow, and the section of our boat was nearly equal to that of the canal. The outside width of the canal was about four yards, and there were many very sharp curves in it, so getting our unwieldy tub along was very hard work. Zurbriggen and I lent assistance, and I took to bossing, so we managed to crawl ahead, but very slowly. Some of the curves of the canal were of such small radius that both ends of our boat stuck into the banks at once, and we had to break out pieces from the banks to enable us to proceed. At 9 a.m. we

The Karakorams and Kashmir.

reached the spot where the canal joins the Jhelam river again — that is, the upper Jhelam river above the Walar lake. The immediate junction is the very worst spot to get through on the whole way. I don't believe the natives would have got that boat through by now if we had not helped. The native rope for hauling is by no means reliable. Once when the decisive moment had arrived, and Zurbriggen and I were hauling like grim death, the rope parted, and back somersaults of an involuntary description were the order of the day. It took us over half an hour to do the last dozen yards, but at last we got through, and then we had a very welcome breakfast.

Up the river the towing, &c., was again of a comparatively easy character, and our progress till the afternoon was smooth and uneventful. At 5.15 p.m. a strongish gust of wind removed the thatching of our front boat; the natives got vastly excited, and

Srinagar. 15

the female portion of the crew started weeping violently—why I don't know, as all the damage done was repaired in less than an hour, and only involved the expenditure of a few bits of straw rope. Then we were off again, and arrived at our present stopping place at dusk. We are at the lower end of the town of Srinagar, and here we stop for the night. To-morrow we shall go up to a more convenient and sanitary place above the city, where to camp for some time while getting ready for another start.

II.

SRINAGAR, THURSDAY, APRIL 7.

ON Sunday (3–4–92) we left our camping-place at 6.30 a.m., and came slowly up through the town, turning up a side stream and arriving at a stopping place at 9 a.m. ; but in the afternoon we shifted to another, where we are now.

On the way up through the town we were quite a procession, for we were accompanied by any number of native dealers in boats offering everything in creation. The persistence of these natives is truly remarkable —profanity affects them but little ; even

Srinagar. 17

personal violence fails unless it is very forcibly applied. Even as I am writing we are surrounded by a crowd of natives who are trying to sell us anything and everything.

We are here at Srinagar for some days to complete arrangements. We are all flourishing, and it seems to me that there could not be a more delightful way of spending a month or two than by pottering about in this neighbourhood. It is a very lovely spot. At first, however, till I got used to his ways and discovered his good points, I found the native dealer very objectionable. He is difficult to avoid. I begin to see the truth of the proverb which associates speech with a silver currency. The first day I was here I found a shady, grassy spot by the river bank, and settled down to write—and smoke—in great content. But very soon there came to me two natives, who spread bales of cloth around me, and conversed volubly in an unknown tongue. They were

18 *The Karakorams and Kashmir.*

followed almost immediately by three who had various odd chairs, who followed the example of the first comers. Next came a man in the leather-goods line, a couple of men with copper pots, and I don't know how many more. And all of them chattered away as if their very life depended on it. I first of all replied in polite English, but they did not understand. It is, however, curious to note that when my language ceased to be polite, though it retained its Anglo - Saxon character, they obviously understood — but they did not clear off. Ultimately I retreated on board our boat, and told our bearer to exterminate any natives who might turn up. In the course of the last few days, however, I have bought some things. The true Kashmir shawl is—alas!—almost a thing of the past hardly any being made now; and those that are made want millionaires to buy them. An inferior imitation is made in large numbers, but it does not appeal to me.

Srinagar. 19

The place is, however, a great one for fine silver and copper work. I bought a silver claret-jug, two splendid carved walnut tables with copper ornaments, some precious stones, and various oddments. The process of purchase was similar to the one I had found at Abbotabad, and it interested me very much to explore the New Bazaar—a most amusing place to do shopping in.

It is a great square building with open courtyards in it, the building itself consisting of innumerable little houses in which the ground floor is usually devoted to manufacturing. The shop proper, where you look at the goods for sale, is generally on the first floor, and you have to go up some remarkably-constructed stairs to arrive there. The main entrance of the bazaar is by stone steps leading up from the river, and I went there by boat. In fact, almost all important traffic is done on the river, and it is the centre of business. Mark Twain's lightning-conductor man is a quiet and retiring indi-

20 *The Karakorams and Kashmir.*

vidual compared to the native shopkeeper. As soon as I set foot on the lowest step in getting out of my boat, I was surrounded by a yelling crowd of native shopmen, each of them shouting out that he was the only honest man there—that he sold cheaper and better things than anybody else—that all the others were thieves and rogues, and such-like. It was really most interesting and amusing as well, though in one sense not pleasant—I mean the olfactory one. But I saw some very lovely specimens of work, and one can get them at a very cheap rate if one has sufficient patience to go on bargaining for hours for any single lot. So far I have not reached bottom prices, though I have several times got things down to less than a fifth of the price originally asked for them ; but it is a very exhausting pro-cess. All things of native manufacture are exceedingly cheap according to our notions. But then native labour, whether skilled or unskilled, is very cheap. It seems to be

Srinagar. 21

paid at the rate of $1\frac{1}{2}$ to 4 annas per day.[1] Some of the skilled workmanship is very remarkably good, but much is already being spoilt by bad attempts at European imitations. The true native articles show for the most part a very considerable artistic taste, but the European imitations are truly hideous. The native is curious in his tastes when he gets on to unfamiliar articles. Our Ghurka soldiers, for instance, have all conceived a violent liking for certain red cotton handkerchiefs of mine— articles such as the British workman likes to carry when he puts on his extra Sunday attire, the cost thereof varying from $2\frac{3}{4}$d. to $4\frac{3}{4}$d. If these Ghurkas behave very well I will present them with one apiece.

How many thousand boats there are in and about Srinagar I cannot estimate, but the handling as far as I have noticed at present is very nearly as bad as it can

[1] There are 16 annas to 1 rupee. In 1892 about 16 rupees = £1, so that 1 anna = about 1d.

The Karakorams and Kashmir.

possibly be. The mechanical bump certainly does not seem to be developed about these natives—what pieces of machinery one sees are carefully constructed to give the minimum of result with the maximum of power expended.

Our boat crew—or rather the crew of both our boats, as they are of joint ownership—consists of a sort of family party. The chief clan consists of three brothers—called respectively Gofara, Esisa, and Subana—who look very much alike. They are all three well-developed, fairly strong looking specimens, with faces expressive of considerably more intelligence than they possess—judging, at least, from the way they handle their boats. Then there is the father of the family, called Jumma, a fine-looking old chap; and his wife, who looks as if she were not descended from the Witch of Endor, but that very lady herself. Then there is Mrs. Gofara and a younger sister, whether of Mrs. Gofara or of the clan I am unable to determine. She

Srinagar. 23

is a girl of, I should think, fifteen ; rather nice-looking, at least when she is in a pleasant humour ; but when she is in a bad temper she looks, and I imagine talks, like a perfect little fiend. Then there is a little blind girl (about ten), and a boy-baby in arms with a very healthy lung development. The natives appear to object very strongly to my writing down the names of the female members of the crew. I cannot discover the reason for this superstition. Finally, there is little Dolda. The latter three appear to be children of Gofara. Dolda is a sweet little girl of about six ; at first she was rather solemn and sad-faced, but she has struck up a great friendship with me, and turns out to be a most merry, mischievous little imp. She considers it the primest fun in the world to splash me with water, and when she thinks I have suffered enough she picks some flower or other from the bank and presents it to me.

We did nothing the first two days. On

24   *The Karakorams and Kashmir.*

Tuesday (5-4-92), Conway, McCormick, and Roudebush (who has rejoined us), left in the smaller of our two boats to go up the river to visit some ruins somewhere or other. I remain here with Zurbriggen awaiting our luggage train.

Our original plan has been modified. When our luggage and stores arrive they are to be divided into two parts ; one is to be sent to Askole, and the other to Gilgit. We intend to travel by Astor and Gilgit up to Hunza, and start there doing some climbing. Then we intend to work across to Askole—if practicable, by the R Zong La (La = Pass) ; and after doing what we can there in the way of ascents and exploration, particularly attacking K2, to return by some other way to Astor and ultimately back here. These are our present plans—of course, liable to much alteration ; but our next journey from here will be to Gilgit, and we shall follow the ordinary road subject to any variations that may occur to us as advisable on the way.

Srinagar. 25

Yesterday the expedition found its first " Edelweiss." Zurbriggen was the man whose eye first spotted it. As far as I can see, it is exactly like the Swiss Gnaphalium Alpinum in appearance, but it has a distinctive scent about it that is quite noticeable. Of course, the flowers, as is only natural at this time of the year, are very small, averaging rather less than the size of a sixpenny-piece.

III.

BANDIPUR, THURSDAY, APRIL 14.

OUR mule train arrived at Srinagar about noon on Thursday last (7–4–92), and later on in the evening our wanderers returned, having visited the ruins they wished to see. I was very busy arranging our luggage. It had to be divided into the two lots which are to go to Askole and Gilgit respectively, and most of it had to be repacked for carriage by coolies. The favourite native way is to have things packed in a "Kilta." This is a frame of basketwork covered on the outside with leather; it is about the shape of an Italian

Bandipur. 27

oil-jar, about 20 to 26 inches high, and has a lid secured by three very roughly-made chains. The load carried, per man, seems to be a very uncertain quantity ; but as far as I can gather 60 pounds seems to be the usual average. Of course the amount carried varies very much with the conditions of pay ; when the men are paid piecework there is naturally a corresponding result.

One amusing incident happened which shows that the native is in some respects like Bret Harte's Heathen Chinee. The local butcher has one of those ordinary spring balances, known as a "butcher's terror," which he weighs his joints on. Our bearer came to me with a joint which had been weighed in his presence as being 24 pounds, but he looked upon it with suspicion, and came to me about it. So I produced my own " terror," and found the weight to be 18 pounds ! Verily, the native understandeth the art of weakening the spring of the " terror."

28   *The Karakorams and Kashmir.*

We did no work on Monday, which was the Hindu New Year's Day, and we celebrated it by laziness. We took a boat, and started at 11.30 a.m. by way of the Dal lake. This lake has, at its entrance, a gate or lock which is a good one, and not the product of native ingenuity. It is arranged to work automatically and close when the lake falls to a certain level. We first of all visited an old mosque, which had nothing specially noticeable about it, and then went on (by boat) to the Shalamar Bagh (= the garden of the abode of love), a garden celebrated in poetry, where we had lunch. There are very many other fountains and other water devices there. The natives offered each other and us branches of lilac, which is the native equivalent of " A Happy New Year to you."

Then we went on to some other gardens, the Nishat Bagh (= the garden of gladness) —this represented the equivalent of Hampstead Heath on a Bank Holiday, and was

Bandipur. 29

just about as crowded as could be. We returned at about 8 p.m. and found Bruce, who had arrived.

Yesterday we finished the division of our luggage, and sent off the bulk of it to Askole. The rest we took with us, starting by boat at 8.45 p.m. ; we went down the river during the night, and crossed a corner of the lake during the morning, arriving at Bandipur at 10.15 a.m. Here we left the boats, and from now our progress will be marching, there being no other convenient available means of locomotion. Orders had been sent on in advance that a sufficient number of coolies (to act as porters) were to be ready for us there ; but it took some time to get the requisite number together, and we did not start till nearly 1 p.m. Then we did our first half-day's march, of about four miles, which brought us to our present situation— a convenient camping-place situated by the side of a clear mountain torrent. We are here about 5,200 feet above sea level, and

30   *The Karakorams and Kashmir.*

there is still plenty of snow on the hills around.

We are all going together till we reach Gilgit, where Roudebush and Dickin will stop and shoot during the summer; and we hope to pick them up again somewhere on our return at the end of the season. We have three Ghurkas with us, also three shikaries (a sort of native hunter), and any number of ordinary coolies; some of the latter are coming with us by the month, while others will go from village to village. Then we also have our general factotum, the "Bearer," and several inferior sprites acting as his assistants.

IV

BURZIL, WEDNESDAY, APRIL 20.

WE started from our first camp near Bandipur on Friday (15-4-92) at 5.45 a.m., and walked up about 4,800 feet to our next camp, Tragbal Chok, a little hollow on a ridge with a small tarn on it. There were odd patches of snow around at this elevation, and for the first time since leaving England, I had a drink of really clear cool water. At that spot there was a very good view of Haramuk (16,903 feet high), a mountain which from this side appears to be an easy ascent, something like the ordinary way up Monte Rosa.

32 *The Karakorams and Kashmir.*

Haramuk is the last peak at the western end of the Himalaya range that has glaciers coming down from it. In character it is really a big mass and hardly a distinctive peak.

Bruce and Zurbriggen left us in the early morning. They are off on a shooting expedition, and will rejoin us at Astor while we potter along slowly with the luggage.

I am beginning to understand what may be called the Anglo-Indian language. With one exception it all tends in the same direction ; the one exception is the word " hill," which is applied to all mountains, even the highest. Otherwise the Anglo-Indian's words and expressions require a very considerable amount of discounting ; if you knock off about 75 per cent. you get near the truth. Now I had expected to find the coolies here very first-rate porters. The Anglo-Indian had described them to me as wonderful porters, climbers, and everything else. On ordinary ground

Burzil. 33

they were not so bad. But in the last few days I have seen our lot on some easy snow, and that has not given me any great opinion of them—very much the contrary. What I have seen so far of them is that, physically speaking, they are a very ordinary crowd. A fourth-rate Swiss porter could give any of these men points. However, as we are going to change our coolies many times it is quite possible that we may come across some good ones somewhere or other.

On Saturday morning we started early, and went uphill along the "road" (Anglo-Indian for a path, which is occasionally bad and sometimes invisible) very soon reaching snow. The highest point, Rajdiangan, is 11,950 feet high, and commands a fine view. Why the road goes over it instead of taking a lower and easier pass to the left I don't know, nor I think does anybody else. It then descends into the Burzil valley, and runs along the left-hand side of it. The

34   *The Karakorams and Kashmir.*

opposite side would be much safer. The path we went along must be lively earlier in the year ; we crossed *débris* of more than one hundred avalanches ! We were several hours on the snow on this day. We camped at Kanzalwan (7,900 feet), at the junction of the Burzil and Kishen Ganga rivers, and the next day we walked up the Kishen Ganga valley. At first it formed a narrow gorge, with much avalanche *débris* to cross ; then it widened out considerably at Gurez, which is the collective name of a portion of the valley containing some half-dozen small villages, and a Kashmiri fort, by which we camped (8,290 feet). The scenery here exactly resembles the Swiss, but is on a larger scale. The native huts are built in the same way, of rough pine logs, the only difference being that the roof consists par- tially of bark, instead of entirely of stone. Even the very smell of the villages is the same, but that also is on a larger scale. On Monday we left Gurez with a fresh lot

Burzil. 35

of coolies; a little way above it the valley divides. We went up the one to the left, the Burzil, and camped for the night near a small village called Bungla.

Yesterday we did a very short march of two hours, thirty minutes, to the Mapanun Bag, a storehouse where we camped. Our camp was by the river-side, some six feet above the level of the stream, which here is a considerable mountain torrent. At night our coolies amused us by a "nautch," in which performance the natives sit round in a ring and do a sort of nasal singing, accompanied by clapping of hands, while two chief performers do a kind of shuffling dance in the middle. One of them was a very comic chap indeed, and his attitudinising was very funny.

To-day we started at 5.30 a.m. and continued our way up the valley. After walking an hour and a half, we reached the place where the valley separates into two branches the one running east being the Nagai, and

36 The Karakorams and Kashmir.

the northern one being a continuation of the Burzil, up which we turned, arriving at our camp, Burzil Storehouse (about 11,400 feet high) after three hours, thirty-five minutes walking. Here there is much snow ; in fact, most of the ground is covered with it. We had a slight fall of snow on our arrival, and the weather does not look altogether favourable. To-morrow we are to cross the Dorikun Pass (13,500 feet). We have met a post-runner here, and so I take the opportunity of sending this letter off.

V.

Burzil, Sunday, April 24.

SOON after our arrival here on Wednesday the weather became very threatening, thunder and lightning being followed by a heavy fall of snow, which continued into the night. Our coolies were consequently in rather a sorry plight, the "Storehouse" being merely a rough structure of stones, with an apology for a roof, in which there was not room for a quarter of them. Conway, McCormick, Roudebush, and myself did our best, giving up the large tent to them and crowding together in our two small ones. It snowed hard through the

38   *The Karakorams and Kashmir.*

night, and by 9 a.m. the next morning there were five and a half inches of snow on the ground, and it was still snowing. The day through it snowed on and off, and we were more or less in the clouds all the time. We accordingly determined to send the bulk of our coolies down to Mapanun Bag, where they could find some accommodation ; while we ourselves with the luggage stopped here in camp, and here we are still. Our coolies had orders to return when the weather cleared. At 1 a.m. Friday morning the weather was still bad, and it was snowing slightly ; later on it cleared, and an intense frost set in. Unfortunately the minimum thermometer was not exposed ; inside my tent it was 23° F. at 7 a.m. It remained beautifully clear till about noon ; the sun was very hot, and we managed to dry all our things, which was a great comfort. The temperature rose to 60° F. in the shade, and the snow melted away very rapidly. By 4 p.m., however, it had clouded over again

Burzil. 39

and assumed a threatening aspect, and about 6 p.m. a heavy fall of snow once more set in, which went on for several hours. Towards midnight it left off gradually, but it snowed to some extent all the night. Towards the morning it grew thicker again, and by 7 a.m. yesterday, Saturday, it was again snowing heavily, about three and a half inches having fallen in the night. This was rather a nuisance. If we had a good lot of porters it would not matter, as we could go on all right; but these coolies are a poor lot. I rather think it would kill some of them if we had tried to force the pass in the bad weather there has been; so all one could do was to sit down quietly and curse. My stock of bad language was not equal to doing justice to the circumstances; anybody having a surplus stock of the article on hand in England is requested to send it along here where the article is in strong demand. However, there has been plenty to do. What with attending to repairs,

40   *The Karakorams and Kashmir.*

doing my washing, and other things, I have been very busy during our stay here.

By now I have acquired fame as a medical man ; this fame is chiefly based on the fact that I have successfully treated our bearer, and also the Tesseldar (or chieftain) of Gurez for bronchitis, a disease with which I am very familiar. They were both very simple cases ; and so I, together with their constitutions, managed to effect rapid cures, for which, of course, I got all the credit, not the constitutions. The natives, in common with more enlightened races, are apt to regard the art of medicine as identical with drugging. I am called " Dr. Sahib," and every afternoon my tent is converted into a regular surgery. I am thinking of starting a casebook, and keeping records of them. So far the cases have luckily been very simple— much sore throat and toothache, some fever, &c. Quinine, which they all know, is very much prized by them. There is also a strong run on cocaine ; indeed, I find it quite

Burzil. 41

a good sort of miracle to apply a little of it to the decayed tooth of a native. They want dentists badly ; there are any number of decayed teeth about that want extracting. Chlorodyne, croton oil, and mercurials are also in great request.

I have had several curious medical requests, some of them of a very amusing character. Unfortunately they were a little too confidential to bear relation here. They seemed to think that I had the power of re-endowing them with youth. It is really very easy to become a great medical man here, if one has some small knowledge of the subject ; what I have to do is to tackle only cases of which I feel certain. When I do not know what a man is suffering from, or, knowing it, am unable to cure him, I try to look profoundly wise, and explain to him that I have but few medicines with me, and that I regret that I have not got the one here that is necessary for his complaints.

During the last few days we have been

42 *The Karakorams and Kashmir.*

having a busy time with our instruments, trying to determine time, magnetic variation, and height; and we have made several most unpleasant discoveries. One of the chief objects of this expedition is to survey any new ground we may reach as carefully as possible. I had proposed to bring my own surveying instruments with me, which I know to be good, as indeed they are bound to be, considering their origin.[1] However, another set was offered to the expedition, and it was thought preferable to take these. I very much regret that I did not overhaul them in London. I examined and overhauled nearly everything else, but I unfortunately did not have the opportunity. The result is disastrous.

The fittings in the box containing the theodolite were made partly of unseasoned wood, and in consequence the top level has

[1] They were kindly obtained and examined for me by the well-known authority on Mountain Survey, Herr X. Imfeld.

Burzil. 43

been broken. As, moreover, there are no spare spirit-levels, it is evident that the value of any observations made with the instrument is seriously impaired. The boiling-point apparatus is in good condition, although it is unnecessarily cumbersome. That is, however, a minor and unimportant fault; but our feelings may be imagined when we found that the thermometers supplied with it do not read below 180° F., so that the instrument is useless for heights above something like 19,000 feet. This is all the worse, as our two barometers turn out to be eccentric and self-willed instruments. Conway has been reading them both on various occasions; sometimes the result is that they nearly agree, and sometimes they show a considerable difference, which occasionally has been found to amount to more than half an inch. Neither of them, however, manages to agree with the measurement deduced from the boiling-point.

The brass protractor is in a box of unseasoned wood. This had shrunk to such an extent that, when I wanted to use the protractor, I had to cut some of the wood away before it became possible to get it out of the box.

The prismatic compass is a good instrument, and in perfect condition ; and the levelling staff is also fairly accurate.

The plane table is not flat, and the alidade is crooked in every direction.

I am much disappointed with our instruments ; and so, I imagine, is Conway.

It snowed more or less all day yesterday ; but we have all fairly got the hump over sticking at Burzil, and so we have determined to start this morning, although the weather looks very unsettled and it is snowing slightly. Our coolies have come up again, and are ready to start.

VI.

ASTOR, SATURDAY, APRIL 30.

WE left our camp at Burzil on Sunday (24–4–92) morning to cross the Dori-kun pass. The Tesseldar of Gurez came up to see us off, and brought with him a man who was supposed to know the way over the pass perfectly. The said guide of course turned out worthless, but Conway, armed with a map and a prismatic compass, acted with success as leader, while I took charge of the coolies. The entire way was on easy snow slopes ; it was misty the whole day, and so I did not see much of the scenery.

We started at 8.30 a.m. It snowed gently all the time till we were on the top of the

46 *The Karakorams and Kashmir.*

pass (13,500), and we were more or less in the clouds all the time. The passage up to the top of the pass involved tremendous trouble; Conway had asked me to get the coolies over, and I think he felt a little nervous as to the chances of a breakdown. However, I felt pretty confident of success; and I was well assisted by Roudebush, who showed a pluck and determination which came in very handy. As to our two Ghurkas, the one, Parbir, was of some use; the other, Lilaram, had not been well for some days, and was only of negative value. The Bearer got a bad attack of what is generally called "mountain sickness." We had the greatest difficulty in keeping the coolies going up to the pass. They are the most poor-spirited lot it has ever been my bad fortune to have to do with; repeatedly men threw down their loads and refused to move, but that sort of game does not work with me. The amount of profanity required, however, was really tremendous; I calculated afterwards that it

Astor. 47

must have taken something like ten thousand curses to get them over that pass, not to speak of a considerable amount of personal violence. I got the last coolies to the top about 2 p.m., and then we went down the other side till we reached our camping-place, Chilang, at 7 p.m. It was snow all the way down, but none of it was in really bad condition, while on the way up parts had been fairly soft and bad.

On Monday we continued our way down the valley to Kurim (three and a half hours' walking), where we camped. Most of the way was over snow, and a good many of our coolies showed symptoms of snow-blindness.

On Tuesday the weather was bad ; it rained more or less all the day. We broke our march at Gudhai, where we had lunch ; and in spite of the depressing circumstances Conway, who is a graceful speaker, made a speech in honour of Roudebush, whose birthday it was.

We came down the valley as far as Mykiel,

48   *The Karakorams and Kashmir.*

where we camped. This valley is a very desolate one; in general appearance and character it very much resembles the upper Täsch valley. The first native huts are found considerably below Gudhai, and then there are but few; some way further down there are a few more. The valley is, however, well watered, and there is plenty of grass, and I feel sure that it could support a considerable number of inhabitants. It would be a splendid place for Swiss or north Italian peasants to settle in.

It rained rather heavily during the night and early morning; so we did not get up on Wednesday (27–4–92) till past 7 a.m., when it cleared a little, and although it looked threatening the whole day, rain kept off till the evening. Our day's march here to Astor was of about fifteen miles. Soon after leaving Mykiel I shot a small bird on the other side of the river, and as I wanted to secure it I determined to cross the river to get it, as no native would attempt it. It was a tough-

Astor. 49

ish job, and I only succeeded at the third attempt. I crossed back with comparatively little trouble, as the current was more propitious in that direction. About an hour further down I shot two birds on the opposite bank; but this time I was done. I tried for over an hour at different spots, but I could not manage to get across; and so I lost the birds, which annoyed me considerably.

I am using a gun which belongs to Bruce, or rather to his father. It is a poem—the first gun I have ever used that absolutely and altogether suits me. That gun was clearly meant for me, and it must have been by an accidental mistake on the part of the higher powers that it was bestowed on Lord Aberdare instead.

We arrived here at about 1 p.m., and were received by the Rajah, Bahadur Khan, and his son. They gave us a very welcome lunch consisting of tea, eggs, chaputties (thin unleavened cakes of flour), dried wal-

50   *The Karakorams and Kashmir.*

nuts (excellent), dried apricots, and almonds. His Highness having intimated that some tobacco would be very welcome, we presented him with some.   In the evening I brewed an egg punch, and we celebrated Roudebush's birthday ; he had come of age the day before.   We expected to find Bruce and Zurbriggen ; it had been arranged when they left us at Bungla that they were to meet us here.   Instead of that, however, they have gone off.   The next day, Thursday, it was very dirty weather, raining like anything. Roudebush went off shooting in the early morning, and got the benefit of it.   The camping-ground here is very pleasant ; there are plenty of trees around, which is a very rare feature in this district.   It adjoins the Rajah's house, which, according to the map, is 7,723 feet above sea-level.   There is plenty of fine soft grass, and the Astor river runs in a nullah several hundred feet below us. I have actually, for the first time for many years, got somewhat sunburnt ; Conway,

Astor. 51

McCormick, and Roudebush are at present all beautiful to behold, being in the middle of the peeling and blistering processes.

Yesterday we stopped here, as it was the great Mahometan feast day ; and as all the people in this district are Mahometans, they went in for high jinks in celebration thereof. We stood our servants a feast, and they ate a most alarming amount. There is a polo-ground here, which adjoins the camping-ground, and the Rajah invited us to a "tamasha," which lasted more or less all day. A "tamasha" appears to be the native equivalent for a big spree.

A little before noon the proceedings commenced with a procession, led by the Rajah and his officials, with a band of musicians and a lot of natives. They solemnly, with much music, or rather noise, marched round the polo-ground, and then the distinguished natives and their visitors (ourselves) sat down on some carpets that were spread on the containing wall of the enclosure.

52 *The Karakorams and Kashmir.*

Then they started with a game of polo; this was followed by a nautch; then there was more polo, and so on till darkness set in.

The music was gorgeous in the extreme. The band consisted of half a dozen performers on different kinds of drums, and there was one man who performed on a pipe, a reed instrument which I examined subsequently with a great deal of interest. The pitch, notes, and fingering were nearly the same as those of the chanter of a Scotch bagpipe. It was curiously inlaid with brass, and I made an attempt to buy it, but we did not come to terms. We took some instantaneous photographs of the polo and dancing, but as it was dull and hazy the whole day, I am afraid the result is doubtful.

Our way from here is down the valley till we get to the junction of our river, the Astor, with the Indus; we then strike up the Indus valley till we reach the Gilgit valley, and then go up that to Gilgit. One great convenience we have is that this route

Astor. 53

is at present closed to ordinary travellers. The fact is that it is, and practically has to be, monopolised by Government. There is a pretty large garrison of troops at Gilgit, and they naturally require food. The district only produces just enough for the inhabitants; consequently the food for the garrison has to be brought up from the Jhelam valley, and this, together with the other military stores required, necessitates an amount of transport that the road is hardly equal to. It is at present the only practically available road to Gilgit, which is at a distance of considerably over two hundred miles from Srinagar, and hence the necessity of reserving it for the use of the authorities only. We have, however, permission to travel on it, and as the military transport proper does not get into full working order till later, when the Dorikun pass gets clearer of snow, things are very convenient for us. Extensive works are also going on all along the road with a view to

54 *The Karakorams and Kashmir.*

its improvement. Supplies are everywhere ample, and we can get plenty of coolies.

A " dak wallah " (a kind of post carrier) leaves here to-day and I send this letter by him.

VII.

BUNJI, SATURDAY, MAY 7.

AT Astor we had to engage a fresh lot of coolies, the Gurez men only being engaged up to that place; this time we were also able to obtain a number of ponies, donkeys, and mules, so that our caravan was of a most variegated description. It took a long time to get it under way; and on Saturday last (30–4–92) we consequently did not start till nearly 8 a.m. These coolies carried their loads in a very different way from the Gurez men. The latter used grass rope, and they carried what luggage they had to take in a structure made of two forked sticks held together by straw plaiting, and carried by two straw plaited straps knapsack fashion. They also carried a T stick on which to rest their burden whenever they stopped to rest, which was every two or three minutes. It was almost impossible to keep them going for more than a few minutes at a stretch. When they actually did walk they went pretty quickly, considering the loads they were carrying. This promptly resulted in their getting winded, and then they stopped ; but to walk on slowly and steadily is evidently not one of their gifts.

The Astor coolies, on the other hand, wrap a blanket or some rope round their burdens, and then twist the ends round their arms in sundry curious fashions. It looks a most uncomfortable way of carrying things, but they seem to like it.

Their ropes and cords are made of goat hair, twisted and plaited together ; generally the different strands are made of different coloured hair. The natives here are evidently great at plaiting ; I noticed all the ordinary

Bunji. 57

and square plaits, and also some very curious plaits, new to me, of oblong and elliptic sections, with many strands. The blankets, and also the saddlebags for the ponies, &c., are made of goat hair. On Saturday night we stopped, after a long and weary march, at Dashkin, where there is a small village. On Sunday we started at 6 a.m. Out of this lot of coolies I had as my personal attendant a curious young fellow, who answers to the name of Rangman. He has a goître; it was the first I had seen in this country, but I have seen plenty of them since. There are a good many along this valley. He looks more of an idiot than anybody I have ever seen, but in reality he is a very sharp youth; he would be worth any amount as, say, a cardsharper in England. It much delights his heart when I shoot a bird, and he is great at spotting them for me; a by no means easy task if a bird happens to fall among a mass of scree. His eyes must be remarkably sharp.

58   *The Karakorams and Kashmir.*

My knapsack, which he carried for me, perplexed him a good deal at first. I showed him how it was to be carried by the straps, but this did not seem to be agreeable to him at all. He altered the length of the straps several times, without seeming to get any satisfaction out of them ; at last he discarded them as absurd, and, tying the knapsack to a loop of goat-hair rope, slung the latter round his neck ! And so he walked along, grinning, and looking quite comfortable !

We stopped that day for lunch at a small village called Trubyling, and while smoking after it I saw the first Lämmergeyer I have seen in this country. I took a long shot at him, and managed to ruffle some of his feathers ; but that did not appear to inconvenience him. We reached our camp at Doia Fort at 1 p.m. This valley rather resembles the ordinary Swiss valley, except that everything is on a much larger scale. There is a considerable amount of cultivated

Bunji. 59

ground in it. The way from Astor to Doia is on the left side of the valley, high above the river, and, although in the downward direction of the valley, it ascends higher along the hillside as it proceeds, so that Astor is actually about a thousand feet lower than Doia.

We left our camp at the latter place on Monday about 6 a.m. There are several ways of going to our next camp, and so we separated and went by three different routes. Conway and McCormick went over the Hatu Pir hill, hoping to get a fine view, but they were somewhat disappointed. The Colonel followed the old road. I took to the new road, which, when finished, will be a great improvement. It goes down to the river by an easy gradient, and then is to run for some considerable way close along it till the bridge is reached. The most difficult part of it, along a rock precipice, is, however, not yet made. A large number of men were at work there, drill-

60 *The Karakorams and Kashmir.*

ing holes, blasting, &c. The traverse of this rock-face looked promising from the rock-climbing point of view, but I was unable to attempt it owing to the road-making operations. So I had to go back a little way, and ascend a long way till I struck an old disused path. This skirted the hillside for a while, and then made a very steep descent to the river. All our different routes joined at the bridge, where there is a curious little Kashmiri fort called Ramghat or Shaitan Nara (=the noise of the devil), a rather apt name. It is in a deep gorge, and the Astor river certainly does roar through it. But it cools the air beautifully, a boon I much appreciated, as it was an exceedingly hot day. There were a few Kashmiri troops stationed here. We crossed by the bridge, which looked European, to the right bank of the river, and a little further on, when we found a sufficiently level place, we camped. It was in a little nullah, some little way above the junction

Bunji.   61

of the Astor and Indus rivers.   At our camp
there was a very little vegetation, otherwise
all around there was only loose, desolate-
looking shingle.   We stopped there with
the exception of Conway, who came on by
himself here to Bunji on a pony that had
been sent to meet him.

On Tuesday (3–5–92) we walked our
seven or eight miles here ; all scree, and
we found Bruce, Conway, Roudebush, and
Zurbriggen, so that our whole party was
again united.

This is a very pleasant green patch in
the Indus valley, surrounded by a wilderness
of *débris*, with mountains on both sides,
almost entirely barren of vegetation, rising
8,000 to 10,000 feet above us.   Up the
valley one has a fine view of Rakipushi, a
fine mountain over 25,000 feet high.   To
the south there is a splendid sight—the vast
mountain mass called Diyamir or Nanga
Parbat (=the naked mountain), a most
appropriate name, as the lower slopes, below

62 *The Karakorams and Kashmir.*

the snow line, consist, at least on this side, of dull coloured rock and scree, relieved by hardly any green. The highest point is 26,620 feet high, and as we are here only some 4,000 feet above sea-level, one actually looks up over 22,000 feet !

I doubt whether there is any other place in the world where one can look up a similar height ; I certainly have never heard of any.

We found three Englishmen stationed here : Mr. Blaker, of Messrs. Spedding and Co., the contractors who are at work improving the road; Mr. Johnson, the engineer, and Captain Kemball, of the 5th Ghurkas ; in the evening we had a great time with them.

There is also a native fort, with a number of native troops under a Kashmiri Colonel.

It has been intensely hot here. Every day the thermometer has risen to over 90° F. in the shade, and my great treat has been going to bathe in the Indus, the water of which is chiefly supplied by snow and

Bunji. 63

glacier, and is deliciously cool and pleasant. We are told that everywhere over India it is exceptionally hot for the time of year, and I hope it will continue so ; it improves our chances of doing some good climbing.

On Wednesday (4–5–92), Bruce, Conway, Zurbriggen, and Roudebush left early ; the three former to go on to Gilgit to make the necessary arrangements for our further progress, and the latter to shoot. In the afternoon I paid a visit to the native Colonel, who received me most courteously. He was evidently a perfect gentleman.

This was the first time I had an opportunity of meeting and conversing with an intelligent native of the higher classes. He understood English somewhat, and had an assistant who was master of it and acted as interpreter when any difficulty arose. The conversation was most interesting, and at the same time most amusing to me. It showed me how very vast the difference is between Oriental ideas and our own.

64 *The Karakorams and Kashmir.*

He commenced by explaining to me that the ways and customs of Englishmen were strange and but little known to him, and therefore he begged that, should he say anything that seemed discourteous to me, I would put that down to his ignorance of our customs, and not to his intentions, for he much appreciated the honour of my visit and wished to treat me with every consideration.

Of course I fully agreed to this, and asked him to look upon any remarks I might make in the same light.

He then said that often and vainly had he tried to understand the strange ways of the white sahib log (=master people), and perhaps my great and exceeding wisdom might make them clear to his ignorance.

I replied that I would do my best to clearly and truthfully answer any questions he might put.

The following is the substance of our conversation, leaving out much metaphor and more compliment :—

Bunji. 65

Did I work for a living?—Sometimes.

Had I any money?—Some.

Was I earning any money at present?—No.

Was I in government employ?—No.

Why was I there, then?—Because I liked travelling.

Who paid me to travel?—Nobody.

Had I been ordered to travel there and nowhere else?—No, nobody had the right to order me about.

So I travelled out of free choice?—Certainly.

Did I know the character of that district before coming there?—Yes.

Then why, if I wanted to travel, did I go about in such an uncomfortable district? Why did I not travel in, say, the valley of Kashmir, where everything could be obtained that man might desire?—Because I preferred mountains.

But mountains were rough and difficult to travel on, and I had to do much work to cross them.—I liked such work.

66   *The Karakorams and Kashmir.*

But how could I like such work? How could a sensible man prefer to make himself uncomfortable?

Well, that was rather too much of a poser for me, and I certainly could not answer it to his satisfaction. I did my best, but I am afraid I only confirmed the Colonel in his opinion that the strange ways of the white man are past understanding.

Thursday and yesterday I went out geologising, or rather prospecting. A small amount of gold is washed in the Indus river along here by the natives, and I wanted to see if I could find any quartz reefs. Granite, hornblende, and achist was there in abundance, and also some well-marked outcrops of white quartz, but none of the latter that I examined were promising from the gold miner's point of view. There were some better looking ones on one side of the Sai river, which joins the Indus a little above Bunji, but in consequence of the heat it was so swollen by melted snows that I found it quite impracticable to cross.

Bunji. 67

On my return to Bunji yesterday evening I found a wire from Conway, who is at Gilgit, saying that things were arranged and asking us to come on. So accordingly we start this morning.

VIII.

GILGIT, SATURDAY, MAY 14.

LAST Saturday we had breakfast very early, and then Lloyd Dickin and McCormick went on ahead. I had a lot of packing to do, and then had to start off our luggage by a new lot of coolies. These were a little better than the men we have had up to the present, though that is not saying much for them, and I did not manage to get the last one started till after 9 a.m. Bunji is the one green spot in this part of the Indus valley; the new road, which we followed, keeps along the left bank till very near the place where the Gilgit river joins the Indus. The walking is very tiresome

Gilgit. 69

and monotonous, either over loose scree, or else ankle deep in sand. This side of the valley is utter desolation along here, nothing but stones—stones by the acre, stones by the square mile. It was intensely hot. About eight miles from Bunji we reached the spot where a new bridge over the Indus is at present being built; a flying one is in use for the time being. This new bridge will, I think, be rather a fine structure, to judge from the drawings that were shown me. The setting-out, however, I confess, rather baffled me. There we found the engineer in charge of the bridge works, Mr. Maynard, an exceedingly nice and pleasant young fellow, who made us very welcome. We had tiffin with him, and stopped with him till nearly 4 p.m. During our stay with him a very violent wind arose; it came in sudden spasmodic gusts accompanied by much dust, and drove little fragments of stone around in a remarkably unpleasant way. It only lasted for a very short time, but did mischief enough while it continued, carrying Maynard's tent away, and considerably upsetting our tiffin arrangements. When it had subsided somewhat we started, crossed the Indus by the flying bridge, and followed the road by the right-hand bank of the Gilgit river to Big Stone, where we camped. A thing that quite baffles me is the utter ignorance of people here as to distance. Even the road engineers have only the vaguest notions of the distances. The original survey must have been curious. Thus we were told that from the Bridge to Big Stone was six miles. From the bridge the road has a steep ascent, rising 500 feet or so, and it is then fairly level most of the way. But it took me a good three hours and a half to do it, and if it is not a good ten miles I will eat my hat. I have already remarked that Anglo-Indian statements have seemed curious to me ; I think the fact is that Europeans, if in India for any time, tend to acquire native habits in respect to accuracy of statement. As for the

Gilgit. 71

native himself, there is absolutely no dependence to be placed in what he says. He feels bound, in fact, out of politeness, to give you the answer he thinks will please you. This is a specimen conversation which I had near here the other day :—

" Is it far to Gilgit ? "—Intelligent native : " Not so far, your Highness."

" One or two kos ? " [1]—" Yes, your Highness."

" Isn't it three ? "—" It may be, your Highness."

" Is that what it is ? "—" It may be five or six, your Highness."

" Then why the Hades did you say it was one or two ? "—" To please your Highness."

" Now, —— it, what *is* the *real* distance ? " —" Whatever your Highness pleases."

Here is another specimen. We were at a village and inquiring of the appropriate official, the Kotwal, as to supplies.

---

[1] One kos is a little over two miles.

72 *The Karakorams and Kashmir.*

"Any eggs or milk?"—"Plenty, your Highness."

"Sheep?"—"Plenty, your Highness," and so through the list.

We were told there was plenty of everything. So we ordered a lot of things to be brought, and rejoiced in the idea of plenty— milk, eggs, and butter being occasionally scarce; but—well—nothing came. Then we finally sent for the official again.

"Where are the eggs?"—"There are no eggs, may it please your Highness."

"No eggs! Well, where's the milk?"— "May it please your Highness, I cannot find any milk."

"Cannot find any milk? What do you mean? Where are the cows?"—"There are not any cows, your Highness."

"Then what the deuce do you mean by saying there were plenty of supplies?"— "To please your Highness."

Now, how on earth is one to deal with people like this? It is often very amusing,

Gilgit. 73

and occasionally somewhat irritating as well. This, however, is a digression.

We arrived at Big Stone at a little past 8 p.m.; another of the road engineers, Mr. Wilkinson, is encamped there, and we found him just at dinner when we arrived. This is at a spot in the valley that is comparatively level—a sandy level, without a trace of vegetation, the river running in a cutting below which must be two to three hundred feet deep. There is a big stone here five or six yards high—at least so much of it sticks out through the sand. It has evidently been brought by ice. Altogether there is very much evidence of a period in which the glaciers were much more extensive than now; there have evidently been one or more glacial periods here. At present the glaciers seem, according to the few observations that have been made, to be retreating.

We had a very good night at Big Stone; and got up leisurely the next morning, Sunday (8–5–92), having breakfast at 8.30 a.m.

74   *The Karakorams and Kashmir.*

Dickin and McCormick felt disinclined to start, so I left them about 10 a.m., and walked along by myself at a very leisurely pace. The sky was clouded over, so it was cool, and very pleasant to walk ; and occasionally there were a few drops of rain. Wilkinson had left Big Stone in the early morning, having to go to Minawar on business ; I met him on my way as he was coming back. Along the river here one occasionally sees a few natives engaged on gold washing by the river bank rather in the Chinese style. There is a little fine alluvial gold in the river sand, which is washed down from somewhere unknown. It is very poor stuff ; if a day's work results in about four annas' worth it is considered very fair, while eight annas in a day is considered as striking it rich. I saw a number of them at work along this part. When I had gone something like five miles from Big Stone I met some ponies, which had been kindly sent for our use by Dr. Roberts, who is

Gilgit. 75

attached to the Residency at Gilgit. I accordingly mounted one, and rode ahead. Soon, in turning a corner, one suddenly comes upon a green and cultivated tract of land, a small village called Minawar, which is a most marked and refreshing contrast to the stone and sand and general barrenness ever since leaving Bunji.

Just after I had mounted a violent dust-storm arose, very much like the one of the afternoon before; it was a very great nuisance, as it hid mountains and everything from view; in fact, I had some little difficulty in finding the road, which is not at all well marked. Ultimately I reached Gilgit. It extends some two or three miles in length, and looks like a sort of paradise; well cultivated, rich soil, splendid vegetation, and altogether glorious to the eye. The lower mountains cut off most of the view; two snow summits are visible; I think they are Dubanni and Haramosh; but Rakipushi is not visible.

76 *The Karakorams and Kashmir.*

Here I found Bruce and Zurbriggen, and Conway; the latter had been laid up in bed with a bad attack of sickness and diarrhœa, but was recovering again. Quite a stock of letters and newspapers had accumulated for us here.

I was very kindly received by Dr. Roberts, who gave me a bath and a change of clothes (my luggage not arriving till later), which, after the dust I had been through, was exceedingly comforting and refreshing. Conway and I then had dinner at the Residency with Colonel Durand and Dr. Roberts.

I felt as if I was in fairyland; as if the times of the thousand and one nights had returned. There we were, many days' journey away from the nearest civilised spot, surrounded by every comfort that the heart of man might desire. I do not think that a more luxuriously furnished establishment could be found in London or Paris. And then the dinner! By what series of

Gilgit. 77

miracles could such a dinner be produced here? Indeed, I know not.

During the night my inner works went wrong very considerably, just as Conway's had done; evidently we had had something on the road that upset us—probably bad water. I had to take to bed, and was not able to get up again till Thursday. Dr. Roberts put me up at his house, looked after me, and treated me generally with an amount of kindness that I am never likely to forget.

On Monday morning Lloyd - Dickin, McCormick, and Roudebush arrived, and our baggage turned up gradually during the course of the day. From noon onwards it rained quite a considerable amount, a most unusual thing at this place. The total annual rainfall here is remarkably small, probably not amounting to five inches altogether.

Our plans have been altered, and accordingly Bruce, Conway, McCormick, and Zur-

briggen left on Wednesday morning to go
up a side valley called the Bagrot nullah.
Rakipushi is up at the head of this valley,
and they intend arranging a camp as high up
as possible in order to proceed to the attack
of that peak and any other convenient one.

I have pretty well recovered, and start
this morning to join them.

IX.

Dirran, Saturday, May 21.

I LEFT Gilgit on Saturday last (14–5–92) about 6 a.m., on a pony belonging to Dr. Roberts, to proceed up the Bagrot valley and join the others there. The road from Gilgit starts by crossing the Gilgit river just opposite the settlement by a very good bridge built by Captain Aylmer, out of telegraph wire and rough wood only, no other materials being available at the time. It was really an excellent and ingenious structure, when one considers that it was put up by a man who is not a professional engineer.

The road (I cannot refrain from repeating

80   *The Karakorams and Kashmir.*

that the word is Anglo-Indian for what an ordinary mortal would be more likely to describe in language less polite, for in this case to call it even a path is somewhat flattering) then goes down by the left bank for about four and a half miles. Here the Hunza river joins the Gilgit river, and the road divides. The left-hand track goes up the right bank of the Hunza river and is the main road to Hunza and Nagar; while the right-hand one leads to a bridge over the Hunza river, situated something like two or three hundred yards above its junction with the Gilgit river.

This bridge is what is called "a rope-bridge," a very common kind of bridge in this country. It is made of three strong ropes, which are composed of plaited tree twigs, thick grasses, thin canes, or any other convenient material that happens to be handy. The passenger walks on the thickest rope, which is generally flattened in form and from six to twelve inches wide,

Dirran. 81

and rests his hand, if he wishes, on the two other ropes which stretch on each side of him and are of convenient thickness. At short intervals smaller ropes connect the side ropes to the main one. This rope system is hung over the river at its two ends, and accordingly forms a catenary curve. As one goes over it, one therefore modifies that curve; and if it is very windy the bridge will sway somewhat.

A passenger has, in fact, an excellent support, and it is difficult to see how anybody could lose their balance, or run any risk in crossing such a bridge, always assuming that it is sufficiently strong. The usual native practice, I believe, is to put up the bridge, never repair it, and go on using it till it breaks. Then in course of time a new one is made, and as for the unfortunate individual or individuals who were on the bridge when it broke—well— it was their "kismat" (fate) to die; and so they died—and that is all. So in order to

The Karakorams and Kashmir.

obviate any risk to himself, the white man tests the efficiency of the bridge in practice by sending a number of loaded coolies over it before venturing on it himself—the coolies, though timid enough under other circumstances, having no objection to rope-bridges. I had heard many tales of the strain to the nerves involved in crossing them. Why that should be so I did not altogether see before I tried one ; now that I have tried I can understand it even less. Considering both the substantial test to which the bridge is subjected before being entrusted with a precious European life, and the aid to mental serenity and physical balance which the side-ropes give, it seems to me that only people afflicted with constitutional giddiness could be affected by them ; and such people are certainly out of place in this part of the world.

The particular bridge here is called the Dewar bridge ; at the further side is a small native fort, and a village of the same

Dirran. 83

name. Here I left Dr. Roberts's pony, rope-bridges not being practicable for him; so I crossed alone and engaged a native pony on the other side. This animal had a most remarkable native saddle, which made me feel as if I was continually turning a corner. The path was semi-decent as long as it kept along the Gilgit river, but it very soon turned off to the left up the Bagrot valley. I rode as far as the first village (called Sinakar) in this side valley, and found the path for the most part remarkably vile. With very few exceptions one could not go at anything beyond a slow walking pace, and occasionally it was so bad that I had to dismount. At the village I made a short stoppage, and left there at 2.30 p.m. on foot. The path up the valley from here is mostly very rough, but there are many cultivated parts along it, with occasional small villages. A glacier (the Bagrot) sweeping down from Rakipushi seems to

84 *The Karakorams and Kashmir.*

block up the end of the valley; but it does so only in appearance, for it just fills up a bit of the valley as it sweeps into it sideways. I went to the right of it along the moraine, and just above where the glacier enters the valley there is again cultivation. I then bore to the left, going up along the left bank of the glacier, and ultimately found the others at camp here at Dirran. I arrived about 8 p.m.; but I was rather handicapped for the next few days, as Conway had forgotten to leave any food supplies available for me on the road. My stomach, weakened with its recent troubles, had to go without food all that day, and resented the omission by re-lapsing into a troubled condition; which, however, is now slowly disappearing.

This camp is situated on the left-hand bank of the glacier, some nine thousand feet above sea-level. It is upon an old moraine, covered with big pine-trees. Between us and the glacier there is a

Dirran. 85

hollow, and then another old moraine, much higher, also covered with big trees. In the latter moraine, just opposite our camp, there is a big gap through which we can see the glacier. Between the moraine and the glacier there is a lake ; and the gap in question has evidently been formed by the repeated bursting of that lake.

At present there is still a good deal of recent snow about, and till it is cleared off, which certainly will take some days, mountaineering proper on higher summits will be impracticable.

Bruce, Conway, McCormick, and Zurbriggen went off on Tuesday morning to pitch a camp on the other side of the glacier, while I remained here, with plenty to do. The weather at the time looked distinctly promising ; but on Wednesday afternoon it grew somewhat stormy, and at 6 p.m. there was a little thunder, and much wind. During the night, however, it cleared up ; the temperature fell rapidly, and in the

86 *The Karakorams and Kashmir.*

early morning there was an intense frost. At 7 a.m. on Thursday I went up to the top of the moraine opposite the camp, and at once saw a party on the snow facing me, just a little below the pass opposite us. This pass is called the Uchubagan Pass ; at present there is still a good deal of snow on and below it, but later in the season it is free and used by the natives as the means of communication with the valley on the other side. It is the best way thither. I fetched my telescope, and saw that the party consisted of three. Two of them seemed to get on very well, but the third lagged behind a good deal and appeared to be rather done up. The snow seemed to be rather bad in places, and I noticed that they made a considerable *détour* to the left, probably to avoid bad snow. They arrived at the top of the col at 7.45 a.m., and then went out of sight. I looked out for them several times subsequently, but did not see them. In the early morn-

Dirran. 87

ing it was perfectly clear, but towards noon it clouded over and a few drops of rain fell.

About 11 a.m. I went over to the glacier lake and had a very enjoyable bath. There are a lot of small icebergs floating about in it, and while I was bathing, the biggest one, visible above the surface to about the size of a chalet, turned over and broke into three pieces with a loud crash. It made quite a commotion, and the surface of the lake was thrown into considerable waves.

In the afternoon I walked up along our moraine for about two hours in spite of a fair amount of rain, hoping that it would clear. I lit a fire at the highest point I reached, and dried myself. Here I stopped for a long time. Never was weather more exasperating. The clouds would become thinner and thinner, till I thought that in another five minutes it would be quite clear; then suddenly they were as thick again as at first. This most aggravating process was repeated time after time, and so I was dis-

88   *The Karakorams and Kashmir.*

appointed in my hope of having a good look at Rakipushi. At last approaching darkness induced me to return to camp, and there I found Zurbriggen, who had arrived back in the meantime. He brought the unpleasant news that Bruce is not well; he is having a return of Burmese fever, and is likely to be laid up at least a week. The party of three which I had seen in the morning had consisted of Conway, McCormick, and Zurbriggen, and from the pass on which I saw them they ascended a minor peak to the north to do some surveying. But when they reached it they found that unfortunately most of their view was cut off, and so Conway in disgust called it by the rather apt name of the " Serpent's Tooth." Yesterday Conway and McCormick returned, accompanied by Dr. Roberts, who has come to. stay a little time with us.

One of our Ghurkas, Lilaram, has been rather unsatisfactory; he was already ailing when we left Srinagar. Consequently he

Dirran. 89

has been sent down to Gilgit, where some men of his regiment, the 5th Ghurkas, are stationed, and we are going to have another man to replace him.

This camp is a wonderful place for flies ; one would almost think the days of Egypt had come again. I am pretty fly-hardened ; my education in that direction took place in South Africa. Conway, however, I regret to say, is different ; flies settling on him irritate him fearfully, and so he suffers.

X.

GILGIT, SUNDAY, MAY 29.

LAST Sunday (May 22, 1892) Conway, McCormick, and Zurbriggen left Dirran, to go and establish a camp at Gargo. Dr. Roberts and Roudebush accompanied them. I remained at Dirran, engaged in mechanical pursuits. Bruce's gun and one of the cameras had been injured, and I had to put in much work on them. Excepting Tuesday, it rained and thundered every day.

Bruce joined me on Wednesday, having perfectly recovered; and on Friday he and I moved the remainder of the camp up to Gargo. The Bagrot valley has two main branches; down one comes the Bagrot

Gilgit.

glacier, by which was our Dirran camp. We went down a little bit, and then up the other branch, of which a very considerable part is well cultivated, and in it there is a flourishing village called Sat. The path went on for some two hours through rich cultivation, and then we reached the end of the Gargo glacier; beyond this there was some two and a half hours of tiresome walking on moraine-covered glacier, and then we struck the camp, about 11,000 feet high, which was situated in a hollow between an old moraine and the present one on the left-hand bank of the Gargo glacier. There we found Conway, McCormick, and Zurbriggen, together with Roudebush, Dr. Roberts having in the meantime left for Gilgit. Roudebush was supremely happy. He had at last managed to shoot something—a bear—and that feat was, of course, the prevailing subject of conversation. Otherwise there was not much news. The weather with them, as with me, had been mostly abominable, and surveying operations had consequently made but little progress. We were all in a more or less humpy condition in consequence. Various plans were discussed, but as they all depended on the weather their prospects seemed somewhat shaky. In the night it snowed heavily, and by yesterday morning there were about four inches of snow on the ground at the camp. Accordingly, at 10 a.m., McCormick and I left for Gilgit, taking Roudebush with us and leaving the others, who intended to try their fortunes for some days longer up the Gargo glacier.

McCormick and Roudebush rather rushed on; I followed more comfortably, getting to the end of the Gargo glacier at 11.30; and then walking down through the fields and village, reached the end of the Bagrot glacier at 1 p.m. Just before I arrived I heard a loud crash. On arriving at the spot I found that this was due to the collapse of the terminal arch under which the

Gilgit. 93

stream issued. A very considerable breakdown had taken place. I went on a little bit, and then sat down and had a pipe. I had found a very convenient sheltered spot, and a shower was just coming on. Suddenly there was a very loud report, like a loud clap of thunder; the river rose quite three to five feet in a few seconds; and with a roar brought down thousands of lumps of ice of various sizes, some of them being quite a cubic yard. Many of them were carried down over half a mile before they got stranded. What had happened was this: the broken arch had choked up the exit of the river; the water had accumulated behind the barrier till it had power enough to break through it, and when at last it did so it swept everything away before it. The time from the fall of the arch up to the breaking of the barrier had been about three-quarters of an hour. I then went on. I had lagged behind rather considerably, and at the next village I

94 *The Karakorams and Kashmir.*

caught up McCormick and Roudebush, who were just having lunch, wherein I joined. We then slowly walked on to Srinagar, the lowest village in the Bagrot valley, arriving at 7 p.m., and stopped there for the night. We left this morning at 5.45, and walked steadily down the valley to its end where it joins the Gilgit one. At this point there is a fakir's tomb, rather decayed, where we arrived at 8 a.m. A "fakir" in these parts is a holy man ; and when he dies they bury him, and build a wall round his grave, decorating it with bits of gaily-coloured bunting on sticks.

While we were resting in the welcome shade afforded by these walls, an enormous Lämmergeyer came flying across the valley from the other side of the Gilgit river. For a considerable time this bird gave us a fly-ing exhibition, sometimes coming down very near to us, and at other times, with ap-parently very little effort, rising one or two thousand feet. Then for a time he would

Gilgit. 95

appear to be entirely motionless, suspended as it were in mid-air, and again suddenly sweep from one side of the valley to the other at a quite incredible rate of speed. To see a small bird flying about is already quite perplexing enough to one's mechanical mind, but a large, splendid bird like this is as impressive a sight as I have ever seen.

Really it was an excellent show; he was a most obliging bird, and gave a fine performance of which we had the full benefit. Ultimately he flew away to the north-west, and disappeared behind the Harali ridge. Then we resumed our way. It gradually grew very hot indeed; and from this spot we made but very slow progress. At every shady spot we could find—and there are precious few—we made a stop. McCormick was very unwell, and could only walk with difficulty. At last we reached Dewar at noon. There we had lunch at a beautifully grassy patch, well shaded by apricot and mulberry trees, with vine clinging to them.

96 *The Karakorams and Kashmir.*

We did not leave till 3.15 p.m. We had not intended to start till later; but the villagers informed us that the Hunza river was rising rapidly, and that if we delayed much longer we might find the rope bridge quite impracticable. It had been submerged and somewhat strained since I crossed it a fortnight earlier. So we started then and there. I went over the bridge first, and certainly in the middle the water was within three feet of it. I then sat down and waited for the others. Roudebush followed next; but, for some reason quite unintelligible to me, after one or two abortive attempts he turned back and had to be conveyed across by some of the coolies. As it turned out on this occasion, the incident was rather amusing than the reverse, but I have seen a similar failure at an important crisis lead to tragic results; and it was a relief to all of us when he was landed safely at my side of the river. McCormick came over all right. After we had gone a little way

Gilgit. 97

beyond the bridge, a pony sent by Dr. Roberts met us. Roudebush mounted and rode on ahead here, McCormick and I walking in at a slow rate some time later. It was far and away the hottest time we have yet had. McCormick was quite knocked up, and has had to take to bed.

XI.

GILGIT, TUESDAY, JUNE 7.

THE next three days I stopped at Gilgit, and had a rather enjoyable time, doing repairs and sundry work on equipment things, and going for an occasional ride in the cool of the evening.

On Thursday last (2–6–92) I rode off from Gilgit at 7 a.m. by myself, leaving my luggage and food to be brought on by two coolies, and reached the Dewar bridge at 7.45. The bridge has suffered somewhat ; the river had also risen, and in the middle I just touched water. My way from Dewar was on this occasion to be up the first side-valley, the Manuga one. The

Gilgit. 99

Bagrot is the second one, and the valley I now intended to ascend is substantially parallel with the Bagrot, being separated from it by a ridge of mountains. In this ridge—a good way up—is the Uchubagan pass, reached from the other side by Conway, McCormick, and Zurbriggen on the 19th inst.

At Dewar I was received by the two chief men of the village, Shukur and Sumalik, who seemed very pleasant heathens. They filled me up with milk and fruit while I was waiting for my two coolies from Gilgit. They were only coming thus far, and they did not arrive till half-past ten. They deposited my luggage and then ran off, apparently in a great hurry, without stopping to receive payment or anything. I gathered that they feared that I would compel them to come along further with me, and that the best thing for them accordingly was to make themselves scarce at the earliest opportunity. But they did

The Karakorams and Kashmir.

not neglect to come and collect their pay on my return to Gilgit, and indeed requested bakhshish because they had had to wait!

The officer in charge of the transport at Gilgit had told me that there would be difficulties as men were exceedingly short, that he could only spare me the two men to Dewar, and that beyond that place I should have to arrange for myself.

By good luck there was a youth in the village who could translate, and so Shukur, Sumalik, and I had a talk about the situation of affairs. They told me that there were no men to be had; that all had been impressed for "begar," or forced labour. Formerly it certainly was the custom to impress any number of unfortunate coolies and compel them to work on the Gilgit road, but now that that road is an Imperial one that is of course no longer the case; men at work on it are engaged and paid by the British authorities. There is no doubt that

Gilgit. 101

at one time the system of " begar " was mis-used as a most pernicious system of oppression. There is just and unjust begar. A certain amount of public work is a necessity, such as repairing roads and bridges, carrying letters, &c., and villages are bound to supply men for such purposes. There is no hardship in this; it is practically the same in England, where a man is compelled ‹to do certain work, *e.g.*, act as a juryman or a witness, and is compelled to contribute money (as an equivalent for work) for road repairs and similar objects. In Kashmiri villages, instead of local taxation a certain amount of labour is furnished. In these ways begar is a good and necessary institution, but under a weak and corrupt government it can, and does, lead to flagrant abuse.

However, I knew that begar was out of the question at Dewar, and that that statement was simply an Oriental excuse. I thought it was of no use whatever getting impatient, and determined I would try to play the heathen's own game. By now I am beginning to understand some of his playful ways. I had some tea prepared, and bestowed some on the two chief men, a great treat for them. Then, as we drank tea together, I explained to them that the scarcity of men was sad, and that evidently the blessings of English rule had not yet been fully extended to them, or unjust begar would be a thing of the past in their happy village.

They did not seem very enthusiastic on this subject, and told me that the valley I wished to ascend was bad, very bad, whereas at Gilgit I should find everything my heart could desire ; and that there were no porters.

I said that if there were no porters there were no porters, and that was my "kismat" (fate or luck). However, their village was a pleasant spot, and so I would remain there. To-morrow was also a day, and so was the day after ; and no doubt "Allah," in his great mercy, would send porters later on.

Gilgit. 103

It was my " kismat " to go up that valley ; if the valley was bad, it was bad " kismat ! " But " kismat " was " kismat," and who could dispute its decrees ?

Much more talk in a similar strain passed between us, and then suddenly men were produced, not only the two (to carry my luggage) that I had asked for, but three ; the third one, a rather young man, wished to accompany me in order to " wait upon the Highness."

While this conversation went on I saw a very odd sight : the cows round about us absorbed apricots that had fallen, apparently with much delight. It may also have seemed peculiar to them to observe me in the same congenial occupation.

Finally I started with my three men, some time after noon, up the valley, of which the lower end is very rocky and barren. At 5 p.m. I reached the village of Barhet, which is somewhere about 8,000 feet high. This part has not yet been mapped, and as every-

104 *The Karakorams and Kashmir.*

thing was clouded over it was impossible to take bearings, and I had to fix my position by dead reckoning, which on a mountain path is a peculiarly perplexing and uncertain method.

What I wanted to do was to determine the position of this valley relatively to the Bagrot one, and, if possible, ascend Conway's pass, Uchubagan, from this side. But I felt rather uncertain as to the probability of finding it unless the weather cleared. I stopped at Barhet for the night, and left there on Friday at 7.20 a.m., continuing my way up the valley, and passing successively two small villages called Bure and Derbana. I reached my camp, Surgen, at 12.45 p.m. It is a sort of a high " Alp " with a couple of huts, at present uninhabited. The two huts are situated on a green patch, between an old and the present moraine, on the left bank of a glacier which reaches about half a mile or more lower down. The height there is well over 10,000 feet ;

Gilgit. 105

in fact, I think it is nearer 11,000. The weather was abominable the whole of Friday, and in the night it rained and snowed. So far I had not been able to see anything ; but by dead reckoning I made out that I must be somewhere near the bottom of this side of Conway's pass.

On Saturday it left off raining shortly after 10 a.m., and as it showed faint signs of clearing up I started at 10.40. I had just crossed the stream in the hollow between the moraine and the hillside—about five minutes' walk—when it began pouring again. I took shelter under a tree till 11.5, when it stopped. Then I went straight up the hillside. At 11.35, by way of variety, there was a heavy fall of hail for about ten minutes. I went on steadily, going at a good pace up the slope diagonally towards the north, in the direction in which I estimated the pass to be. And so the weather went on, and so did I, till at last, at 1 p.m., I reached some snow. It was entirely rotten ;

106 *The Karakorams and Kashmir.*

however, I tried to walk on, or rather into it. But as I sank in more than waist deep, I gave it up as a hopeless job. I was a good bit over 14,000 feet high. I sat down on the last rock and cursed the weather. At one moment it became clearer and I thought I could see a snow pass before me, but the fog once more swept up and cut off the view of everything. The weather grew persistently worse, and after sundry varieties of thunder, lightning, hail, and sleet it settled down to steady snow. Finally, I had enough of it, and ran down very rapidly to Surgen, where I arrived at 5 p.m., quite wet through. A fire and dry garments were indeed a comfort. It rained and sleeted all through the night, and early next morning (Sunday) fresh snow was visible on the mountains, as far as indeed anything was visible, down to nearly my level. However, I went up the hillside again in the same direction as before with the idea that it might perhaps be clearer higher up, and at 1 p.m. reached the same

Gilgit. 107

snow which was—if possible—even softer than it had been on the previous day. It was raining pretty steadily; I sat down and waited; at last—oh joy!—for just a few moments the fog cleared and I could see a snow-covered pass in a rounded depression just over me which could, I should think, have been reached in perhaps an hour, perhaps two, from where I was if the snow had only been in good condition. The fog rose gradually; more and more of the rocky ridge to the left of the pass became visible; at last, on a little rocky peak I saw a stone-man, evidently the one put up by Conway on May 19th, and I wildly shouted " Hurrah!"

So I had managed to hit the right pass; and very surprised indeed I was to find my actual position so near my estimated one.

But the improvement in the weather was only for a few minutes, in which, however, I was able to take a few bearings and deter-mine my position, and then once more it com-menced to snow. I hurried down to Surgen,

108 *The Karakorams and Kashmir.*

arriving there once more wet through, at 3 p.m. My natives were exceedingly nice ; my wet clothes of the day before had been dried, and fresh supplies of milk, butter, eggs, and apricots were continually forthcoming all this time. At this period I was using a Mummery tent (so called after its inventor, A. F. Mummery, of Matterhorn and Col du Lion renown), which is really an excellent contrivance — covering 6 feet by 4 feet by 3 feet high. It actually weighs under three pounds, and, considering its lightness, is really quite remarkably weatherproof. The inside of my tent was rather amusing—the number of articles in it which have belonged at various times to various friends was large. To start with, I had an excellent cap, presented to me by T——, which, among other uses, is the best nightcap I have ever struck for cold weather, and is regularly used in that capacity under such circumstances. I also had a second cap, bestowed on me by La—— ; a wonderful

Gilgit. 109

and beautiful fur article, calculated for use when the temperature falls down to somewhere near the absolute zero. Then round my neck I had an old Tartan comforter, contributed by my friend Le—— ; he used to wear it formerly when we went to the "Coster Market" together, and it is quite up to the best Petticoat Lane form. My coat was, strictly speaking, not my coat, or at least was not formerly ; it belonged, or had belonged, to O. W——. I am not quite sure whether he is aware that he has had the distinguished honour of supplying such an excellent article to me. As for my flannel shirt, I am not quite certain as to its pedigree—I think it came to me through D—— ; but as to its original owner, I know him not. Then I had a capital thick-knitted Jersey contributed by Bruce ; a cushion, which I used as a pillow, of which Conway used to consider himself the owner till I mildly but firmly appropriated it, much to his amusement, for use on this particular trip ; a red

The Karakorams and Kashmir.

handkerchief, late the property of the aforesaid Le——, of the kind that the British workmen loves to use—not for his nose, but to carry his dinner in; a pocket-knife which I confiscated from F. W——, and a tobacco-pouch which I once found in a train. The pencil I wrote with used to belong to J——; but in a moment of rashness he left it within my reach, and so of course I annexed it, observing justly that it would be of more use to me than to him. Taking it all round, I was fixed up very comfortably; and if it had not been for the fact that I could not get on with any observations, existence would have been very serene. My powers of cookery were developing tremendously. I had ample supplies, fresh things being brought up by the villagers every day; and I had plenty of first-rate butter.

Butter is very scarce up country in Kashmir, at least in the parts we have been in, and can only be obtained at a few places, and then seldom good. Their butter-

Gilgit. 111

making is primitive : the milk is put in a skin, which is tied up ; and then a man, squatting down, rocks this on his knees till the desired result is obtained. They do not consider butter good till it is many years old, and accordingly store it by burying in the earth. But butter of, say a hundred years or more, to my (uncultivated !) taste is a trifle too elevated. Cheese does not seem to be made anywhere in these valleys.

The natives up this valley were altogether the most intelligent I have yet struck. They actually knew how to make a clove hitch, and fasten tent ropes to pegs with it ! Any one who has seen the fearful mixture of knots people generally in this country tie ropes with, will appreciate how far advanced these folk must relatively be.

It is curious how entirely the natives of two adjoining valleys differ. These men are much superior to the Bagrot ones. This is true also in Switzerland, but not to so

112   *The Karakorams and Kashmir.*

great an extent. Thus the Saas men average distinctly better than the Zermatt men.

On Sunday night it cleared up somewhat, and the moon was visible ; at daybreak yesterday it looked promising, so at 4.30 a.m. I started across the glacier, which is somewhat broken up and moraine-covered here. I hoped to take some bearings from the other side—but alas for the fallacy of human hopes! When I was some way across, clouds swept up ; I was enveloped in them and could see nothing, so I returned to my camp, and the way back was not very easy to find. I arrived there at 8 a.m., and started breakfast, and as the weather grew worse rapidly I determined to go down to Gilgit. At 9 a.m. it commenced to snow ; there were violent gusts of wind, and the needle of my aneroid moved to and fro in a most suggestive manner. I started at 9.45, and reached Bure at 11.35 ; there I stopped a short time for lunch, the weather

Gilgit. 113

clearing somewhat. But on the way further down a fresh storm broke, and a peculiar variety of hail fell which was more like pieces of snow névé than ice. I arrived at Barhet at 1.15 p.m. pretty wet. A wind blew in violent gusts, and it was quite impossible to pitch the little tent, so I had to take refuge in a native hut, which, for a wonder, was singularly free from smell.

In the afternoon as I sat writing there, keeping a side eye on my lunch, which was cooking by my side, I noticed considerable excitement among the crowd of natives who, as usual, sat watching me. They all left the hut ; and as considerable talking went on outside, I went to see what was the matter, and I saw a very remarkable sight.

On the opposite side of the river the hillside is fairly precipitous ; and facing the village, but a little higher up, is a big cave in the rock, and underneath it is a stone shoot. This cave is apparently in the solid rock ; it appears to enter horizontally, and

114 *The Karakorams and Kashmir.*

no water comes out of it. The natives evidently seemed to think that something of an unusual character was going on; and so there was. To my surprise, when I stepped out of the hut and looked to see what was the matter, I saw a lot of stones come out of that cave and roll down that shoot; some of the stones were of considerable size, and there were a good many of them. This went on for some ten minutes after I first looked. The stones coming out were DRY, and I cannot at all account for the phenomenon. It would be interesting to go and explore that cave; but its mouth would be somewhat difficult of access. That it was a very unusual event was evident from the great excitement of the natives; but as there was nobody in the valley who understood a single word of any of my languages, and I was only just beginning to learn the first few nouns in theirs, I could not discuss the subject with them.

I stopped the night at Barhet. This

Gilgit. 115

morning early it rained heavily, and I accordingly delayed my start till 7.15 a.m., by which time it had cleared somewhat. The path had been severely damaged since I had got up, and we had to ford the river twice to avoid stone shoots which were still active. At one place I saw two dead markhor, which had thus been killed. I reached Dewar at noon; the two head men, Sumalik and Shukur, together with their translating youth, had come some little way to meet me, and seemed very pleased to see me. I had lunch, and discussed various matters with them. They were exceedingly polite and pleasant, and expressed their hopes that I had been satisfied with the " bandobast " (arrangements) they had made for supplying me with food and looking after my comfort, &c. I said their " bandobast " had been excellent, and it was good " kismat " that I had had two such excellent men to make it. I paid the various coolies who had carried my luggage, settled for the food I

116   *The Karakorams and Kashmir.*

had consumed, and also bestowed "bakh-shish" on them. But the young man who had come with me to "wait upon his highness"—which he had done excellently—refused pay or "bakhshish," much to my surprise, and Sumalik and Shukur also said that they did not wish to have any "bakhshish." This was a new development, and it rather puzzled me. I have known "bakhshish" refused in England, but then only when the amount offered was too small. That could not be the reason, as I had named no amount, but merely had stated that I wished to bestow some. My perplexity, however, was soon dissipated. They all three explained that it was in the power of the "Highness" to bestow favours on them which were of far greater value than any "bakhshish" could possibly be; in fact, would I give them each a "chitthi" (anything written is called a "chitthi" or "chit," so in this case they meant a testimonial) to say that they were excellent men, and

Gilgit. 117

that they had treated me very well. So I said I would, and drew up documents in flowery language setting forth these facts, quite grieving that I had to write them on pages torn out from my note-book measuring about six inches by four, instead of on large and imposing sheets. I bestowed these "letters of nobility" on the delighted recipients, and then left amidst a shower of gratitude. I crossed the rope bridge and came on to Gilgit, where I found all the others, who have been there for a few days. They also had succeeded in doing nothing particular. McCormick has been in bed for a few days, but has pretty well recovered by now. Bruce, I regret to say, is again laid up with a return of Burmese fever, and it will be some little time before he is up and about again.

XII.

NAGYR, THURSDAY, JUNE 16.

ON Wednesday (8–6–92), with the exception of Bruce, who is to rejoin us as soon as he is able to do so, but with the addition of Roudebush, we came up the valley of the Hunza river to Nomal, net walking time 6 hours 20 minutes. It was a bad path, and an awfully hot day. On Thursday the temperature was even worse. I have never known a hotter day; we went from Nomal to Chalt (net time six and a half hours), and the path was simply vile—being either loose sharp stones, or more than ankle deep in heavy sand. The Anglo-Indian statements amuse us more than ever. Their

Nagyr. 119

estimates as to distance are based—if, indeed, they are based on anything—on a system not understanded of the common mind. At Gilgit we were informed that it was fourteen miles from Gilgit to Nomal, and eight miles from Nomal to Chalt ; thus making Gilgit to Chalt twenty-two miles ! Now it is true that we did not walk fast, but I certainly estimate the distance to be well over thirty miles ; and the path (which they call in their curious language a fair road) is simply—well—en tirely unfit for publication.

At Chalt there is a little fort, which for years was the furthest outpost of the Kashmir State in this direction. There was a theory that Hunza and Nagyr, the two small robber states which occupy the upper part of this valley, were in a way dependencies or tribu- taries of Kashmir ; but practically these two little territories were independent till they were conquered last winter by our troops. That must indeed have been a wonderful cam- paign ; I do not suppose that any other campaign has ever been successfully conducted in a country with such enormous natural difficulties ; and I believe that, now that the district has been opened up, good roads will in time be made through it. However, that is a thing of the future. But the heat is remarkably oppressive here, chiefly from the effects of reflection from the bare rock. There are only very few green spots here and there where side streams can be utilised for irrigation and subsequent cultivation of the irrigated ground.

The night was not much more comfortable than the day had been, for Roudebush had left his tent behind at Gilgit, and at Conway's request I gave up to him the expedition tent which had been intended for my use. This, however, was only a minor inconvenience ; but it indicates the mistake of bringing inexperienced men on expeditions of this kind.

We left Chalt on Friday at 6 a.m., and half an hour beyond it crossed the Hunza river, proceeding along its left bank. There

Nagyr.

121

is a good bridge at this spot built by Aylmer; like the one at Gilgit, it is of telegraph wire and timber. The Hunza river just above this bridge makes a sharp bend round a corner, and there is a big shoulder of precipitous rock where the river sweeps round it. The path from the bridge goes over this shoulder—a steep ascent of about 1,000 feet; and from near the top of it we had a magnificent view of Rakipushi, which stands up by itself high above the mountains surrounding it. Its shape, as seen from here, reminded me rather of one of the aspects of the Weisshorn. We also had good views in other directions, and in the dim distance mountains were visible which looked to me unexpectedly high.

But the contrast between the different parts of the valley is the most striking feature visible from here.

The valley so far runs approximately south and north; it is generally narrow, and in places it is more like a gorge than anything

122 *The Karakorams and Kashmir.*

else. Except at rare spots, all is rough rocky or sandy ground, surrounded by barren precipices of rock, with hardly any trees.

The upper valley above this point runs roughly west and east ; it broadens out very considerably, and on both sides there is abundance of welcome green with many villages close together. The north side of the valley forms the state of Hunza, and the south one that of Nagyr. There is much cultivation in the lower levels, and up above the hill slopes have a good deal of timber on them. It has a look of richness and prosperity about it ; in fact the district is like a green oasis surrounded by vast stretches of rugged and desolate rock. It would be difficult to find a finer view of a valley than the one visible from this shoulder.

On the further side of it there is a steep descent of nearly 800 feet, and then a levellish path of some five or six miles cut occasionally by a deep "nala" (into which we

Nagyr. 123

had to déscend, and then ascend the other side) took us to the outskirts of Nilt, which was the chief centre of the recent fighting. Plenty of signs of it were left visible in the line of breached and blown-up forts, &c.

Nilt joins on to Gulmat, where we arrived at 4.30 p.m. and camped. We stopped here during Saturday; one of our Ghurkas had been in the fighting, and during the morning he took me round and explained everything to me.

In the afternoon I went and watched the native smith, who indeed was a wonderful man. His forge was under a tree, and consisted of four lumps of stone laid on the ground. Charcoal was the fuel; and two goatskin bellows worked by an assistant youth gave a very irregular blast of air. He had a hammer of the shape loved by the French fitter [1]; his anvil was

[1] The hammer used by the French fitter has a square head with a flat face. The English fitter uses one with a circular head, and the face is rounded a little.

124 *The Karakorams and Kashmir.*

very small, and the rest of his gear could almost have been carried in a waistcoat pocket.

Now one of our knives, an ordinary table-knife, had had its blade snapped in half, and I took it to him in order either to repair it myself with the use of his forge, or let him repair it under my supervision. He said he could do it, and so I told him to go ahead. I expected that he would proceed to braze the two parts together; I had noticed that there generally was a good deal of brazing in native articles, and another knife of ours that had been broken had been repaired by a heathen in that way.

But there was no question about my supervision; I very soon found out that I was in the presence of a master. To my very great surprise and admiration he proceeded to actually *weld* the two pieces together! Then he hardened and tempered it, ground and somewhat polished it with some little pieces of stone; and finally, when

Nagyr. 125

it was finished, it was not easy to see where the fracture had been.[1]

The whole operation, which was conducted in a true Oriental, leisurely fashion, occupied about four hours; 2 annas had been the agreed price; and when I bestowed 4 annas on the smith and 1 anna on the bellows youth their gratitude was immense.

We were informed by the natives of the place that Bruce was better, and that he was going to start from Gilgit after us. This leads me to mention the fact, well known to most Europeans here, that the natives have a perfectly marvellous way of conveying intelligence across country, with very great accuracy and extreme rapidity. On what system they work, and who works it, is a problem which has puzzled every one; and I believe I am correct in saying, however strange it may sound, that no European has

[1] I regret to say that the knife was lost subsequently; I wanted to preserve it as a curiosity. Welding two such thin pieces of cast steel together requires skill of the very highest order.

126 *The Karakorams and Kashmir.*

yet succeeded in discovering anything about it. Every native, if you ask him, knows, or rather pretends to know, nothing about it. If you ask him whence he obtained the news he just communicated, he will tell you another man has just told him ; and so on. If I had not had personal evidence of the accuracy and rapidity of transmission of their intelligence, under circumstances which seemed conclusive of the fact that some sort of signalling must have been used, I should not at all have thought it possible for a people of such comparatively undeveloped intellect to do it. And how they do it baffles me utterly. How, for instance, can people, of whom not one in a thousand can read or write, signal a name, like Bruce's for instance, which is unknown, if not to the senders, at all events to the receivers of the message ?

We left Gulmat on Sunday at 6.15 a.m. The regular Indian survey extends up to that place, but no further ; beyond, only odd

Nagyr. 127

points have been determined, and so Conway decided to begin making a survey from that point. We came about six and a half miles that day, passing through village after village with much cultivated and rich ground, and native forts all along. A "dak-wallah" (post carrier) passed me on the road, and, according to the habit of his class when they meet a white man, he handed his mail to me to keep what I liked, and tell him as much as I could of the whereabouts of the other addresses. It was really a fine walk ; we crossed three or four rivers issuing from glaciers coming down side valleys, the ends of the glaciers being very near—in one instance within less than a mile. The scenery began to assume a distinctly Alpine character. It was somewhat cloudy, however, that day, so that one only got occasional glimpses of the higher peaks.

We reached Tashot, our camping place, at about noon ; and shortly after our arrival we received a visit from one of the Rajahs of

128   *The Karakorams and Kashmir.*

this part of the world, by name Sekundar Khan, with his son and a suit of about thirty attendants. He was a very fine-looking young man, with a martial bearing and a handsome, intelligent face. He examined our equipment with great interest; the things that seemed to strike him most were our "crampons" or claws ; and he expressed a desire to possess them, saying that they would be very useful when hunting in cold weather. He had an exceedingly good double-barrelled express rifle (Manton), which he showed us with a good deal of pride. I understood that it was a present from the English Government. Of course we had tea together, and there was a "tamasha." The royal band of three, one piper and two drummers, struck up a tune, and sundry dignitaries and others danced around in their peculiar fashion.

It was here that I saw the first Pamir sheep I have ever seen. This animal, which is bred all over the Pamirs, that district of

Nagyr. 129

many disputes, is a large, well-formed sheep; but instead of having a tail, it has a curious flap-shaped appendage. The one we saw was a white ram; the flap was about 8 inches wide, 10 inches long, and 2 to 3 inches thick. It was rather square in shape, the lower corners being somewhat rounded off. Of course this appendage looks much bigger, for, like the rest of the animal, it is covered with thick wool. This flap is considered by some natives specially good eating; but they asked the prohibitive price of 10 rupees for the animal, and so we did not purchase it. The ordinary sheep of the country varies a good deal in price; at Bagrot we paid 2 rupees 8 annas; at Gulmat, 2 rupees; at Tashot, 1 rupee 8 annas; and here at Nagyr they charge us 3 rupees for one, but then their sheep are a good deal better than the average on the way up. We manage to consume just one sheep a day. Of that the best parts are eaten by us Europeans, and the Ghurkas and servants get through the

130   *The Karakorams and Kashmir.*

rest. The coolies in general seldom eat meat, many of them because they do not get the chance, but some from religious motives. No true Hindu eats meat ; and a good many Mahometans, who were originally Hindus, still stick to the practice of not eating it. The staple food of such is "ata" (flour or meal), which they make into thin cakes with water and then bake. The result is called "chaputti" ; it is very tasteless, and has been our substitute for bread most of the way up. It is of course identical, except in so far as the quality of the flour is different, with the Jewish "mátsah" or passover cake. Bread cannot be obtained anywhere except at a European station such as Bunji or Gilgit, and our cooking staff does not seem able, or willing, to make it. We left Tashot at 6 a.m. on Monday, and walked up here to Nagyr, a distance of nearly twelve miles, arriving about 3 p.m. Most of the way is through rich, cultivated country, with numerous villages along both sides of the valley.

Nagyr. 131

All these villages are fortified, and there are numerous watch-towers all along. In almost every village there is a polo ground.

About half way from Tashot to this spot the main valley divides into two big ones; the Nagyr one, which we are in, goes up to the right, and the other, the Hunza one, to the left. Baltit, the chief town of Hunza, is just up above the junction of the two on the opposite side; it is situated near the entrance of a side nala, on the right bank of a stream issuing from it, which is fed by a large glacier, of which the lower end is but little above the town. Just facing it, on this side, is the village of Sumayar. The valley on the way here continued Alpine in character; only the higher peaks were again clouded, and but little visible. The people are much superior to those we have hitherto seen. They understand the use of money and value its possession; their corn is ground in mills driven by water power; and they make very good baskets. They

132 *The Karakorams and Kashmir.*

make matchlocks with rifled barrels, and the boring and rifling are very creditable.

Our luggage was transported very quickly in this district. Previously we had always had one lot of coolies, who went several days' journeys with us. Here, however, one lot only carried it a very short way, to the next village or so; then a fresh lot took it, and so on, so that our luggage was conveyed quite as quickly, if not more so, than we could walk. Then also these men are of a very much better physique, and they hump loads along in a fine style.

This is a big place, and the ground is exceedingly well cultivated. Our camp is situated just at the side of the polo ground, and it is a very pleasant spot. It has one great and very unusual advantage; it is very well planted with Chenar trees, which afford ample shade at all times of the day. As far as I know, no European has yet been beyond this place in this direction, and as it is practically unsurveyed, there is plenty to

Nagyr. 133

do. Existing maps, which are largely based on guess-work, are of course very wrong; on the latest published map, for instance, the town of Nagyr (where we are at present) is placed almost opposite Baltit, on the other side of the river in the main valley, whereas it actually is in the big right-hand valley referred to above, and something like four miles up it. Baltit itself is wrongly placed on the map; it is a good deal west of its supposed situation. A little way above Nagyr the valley splits up into at least four different valleys, or perhaps more. Three of these have large glaciers coming very far down through the cultivation, one actually reaching the outskirts of the town of Nagyr itself. Of course we are regarded with a good deal of curiosity, and since our arrival here we have continually been receiving visits from various dignitaries, such as the " Wazir," or chief minister, and other officials. The old Rajah of the district, Zaper Khan, who can only move about with

134 *The Karakorams and Kashmir.*

much difficulty, and rather looks as if he was a severe sufferer from gout, paid us a state visit; and then various young rajahs or princes, who seem to be of all sizes, ages, and descriptions, but who all appear to possess much liking for chocolate, tea, and tobacco, came at frequent intervals. But means of communication are a little uncertain. They talk a language of their own here. Only a few people understand a little Hindustani; and as our stock of Hindustani (in the absence of Bruce) is limited—consisting only of odd words picked up on the way up—for none of us had any knowledge of it on our arrival in these parts—conversation is naturally somewhat restricted. Anything not of the most commonplace character takes a considerable amount of explaining and gesticulating before it is understood. However, on the whole, one manages a good deal better than would be expected.

It is very difficult to extract any information from them on the subject of routes; at

Nagyr. 135

first they pretended to be entirely ignorant of the existence of any way or road out of the upper·parts of the valley. They evidently cannot quite understand why we should want to know about them, or else they have some objection to our knowing anything ; and so at first they pretended total ignorance. The point is that we want coolies to come with us, if we can get them, right on to Askole. Of course we know well that formerly they used to raid Askole periodically from here, and carry off its inhabitants and sell them into slavery. When asked as to Askole, the Wazir at first said that there was no such place, or at least, if there was, he had never heard of it. Then he said there might be such a place, and gradually admitted that there was such a place. But there was no way there from Nagyr ; there was no way up beyond Nagyr, not to Askole nor to anywhere else. There might have been one formerly, but there was not one now. Or at least if there was one,

136 *The Karakorams and Kashmir.*

it was very difficult. In fact, he believed there was a way, but it was long and wearisome, and of much difficulty. It certainly was not fit for a " Highness." In fact, there were two or three ways out of the valley. I expect that after the worthy Wazir has consumed a few more cups of our tea, and smoked a few more pipes of our tobacco, both of which are great luxuries to him, he will ultimately discover not only that the ways are all right, but that he can supply us with men who know them and are willing to accompany us.

Tuesday we had a day of rest, intending to start next day up the hillside to begin some climbing at last, but yesterday the weather was threatening and became bad ; in the evening it began to rain ; by 11 p.m. it was coming down heavily, and it continued to do so till 6 a.m. this morning. Conway has given up the idea of doing anything on this side of the valley, and accordingly we are going over to the Hunza side to try something there

XIII.

NAGYR, MONDAY, JUNE 27.

WE left Nagyr on Thursday (16–6–92) morning in order to go to Baltit, the chief town of Hunza. There are two rope-bridges to cross; one over the Nagyr river, and the other over the Hunza river. Roudebush very sensibly preferred going down to Tashot, where there is a wooden bridge of the ordinary European type, and went round to Báltit that way, thus avoiding the rope-bridges. I started a little in advance of the other three—Conway, McCormick, and Zurbriggen, and went on till I reached the second rope-bridge, where I waited till the others came. A curious

138   *The Karakorams and Kashmir.*

incident happened there. I had never been present when Conway had crossed rope-bridges before ; but we had discussed them, and he had told me that he had never felt in the least degree nervous in crossing them. On this occasion, however, his nerve failed him, and he had to be roped and conveyed across by Zurbriggen. It is very remarkable how a man, of ordinarily good nerve, will on some single occasion quite lose it without any assignable reason. I have always thought that some such momentary failure may explain the occurrence of some Alpine accidents which otherwise appear quite unaccountable.

A steepish ascent of some 800 feet took us to our camping-ground, situated on a slope a little below the main town of Baltit.

There we found three English officers, J. Mc. D. Baird (24th Punjaub Infantry) and L. Bradshaw (35th Sikhs), who were stationed there, and F. H. Taylor (3rd Sikhs), who had just arrived from some

Nagyr. 139

mission up the Kanjut valley. Seldom have I met a better set of good fellows; we all had dinner together, and a subsequent jollification which lasted deep into the night, or rather early morning.

The weather was rather unsettled, and had been so for some little time. I think, however, that considering the distances our camp has to be moved to arrive at the scene of any possible operations, it would have been wiser to have faced it out, and avoided the waste of time and trouble involved in marching the party up to a camp, only to bring them down again. It is my opinion that by stopping in camp a little longer than we did, and making the most of our opportunities, we could have ascended two or three decent peaks in the last fortnight or so, instead of doing practically nothing whatever. I had frequently been of a similar opinion before; and having regard to the position in which Professor Conway asked me to join the expedition, I think it fair to

140 *The Karakorams and Kashmir.*

record my personal view of the subject. It is, however, right to state that Conway disagreed with me on the point.

The next day, Friday (17–6–92), the Maharajah and his Wazir paid us a visit in the morning ; and in the afternoon there was, as usual, a tamasha. There was a very good game of polo, in which the Maharajah and his Wazir, and also one of the English officers, took part. The royal band, which discoursed sweet music (more or less) during the performance, was this time quite imposing ; it consisted of four pipers and eight drummers.

On the 18th also we stopped at Baltit ; it rained that day ; and early next morning, as it still looked doubtful, Conway preferred to abandon our previous plan of starting up the hillside above Baltit, and determined to go back to the other side of the valley. As it turned out, this was unfortunate, for it cleared up, and the next two days were beautiful, and we might have been able to

Nagyr. 141

do something if we had bivouacked above Baltit as first arranged.

As it was, we went to Sumaiyar, which is on the opposite side. Zurbriggen and I crossed by the rope-bridges ; the others accompanying Roudebush, who went *viâ* Tashot to avoid them, the long, roundabout way he had come.

We then camped at Sumaiyar. The next morning Conway, Zurbriggen, and I, with two Ghurkas, went up the side valley, which is cultivated and fertile most of the way up. We camped on a green meadow about half a mile up above the end of the Sumaiyar glacier, at a height of nearly 11,000 feet, with the intention of moving our camp higher up the next day. In the afternoon I saw the most gigantic avalanche I have ever seen, falling on the mountains on the opposite side. Its mass stopped a long way above Baltit, but the snow dust almost hid Baltit for a few moments from view.

However, on the next day, Tuesday

142 *The Karakorams and Kashmir.*

(21–6–92), Conway decided not to shift the camp, but to walk up first and see if there was a convenient camping-ground higher up. So we walked up along the left-hand side of the glacier till we had ascended rather more than 2,000 feet, and then bore to the left up over the snow-covered glacier for about another 1,000 feet. The mountain face to the south-west was remarkable for avalanches. I counted fifty-seven in seventeen minutes ; they were not very big in comparison to the size of the mountain, but taken by themselves they were so large that it was advisable to give them a wide berth. After a prolonged stay at the highest point reached, we returned to our camp. It had been a very hot day, and I much enjoyed our stroll.

The next day, Wednesday (22–6–92), we went, with light camp kit, carried by coolies, by the same route up the glacier, which is hardly crevassed, and ascends at a gentle angle, till we reached a height of just about

Nagyr.   143

15,000 feet. Our loaded coolies had no objection whatever to going over the snow-covered glacier without being roped, and they readily recognised where crevasses were to be found. Conway, however, with the caution befitting a responsible member of the Alpine Club, roped with Zurbriggen and the two Ghurkas. We made our camp near the right bank of the glacier under a rocky slope, which was surmounted by a little snow hill, the summit of which was about 800 feet above. In the afternoon we ascended this little summit; it was the last point in a ridge running down from a big mountain called Daranshi, of which the highest point was to the east of us.

We expected to have a fine view from the top, and Conway thought it a very fine one; so it was, but only in the line of cloud effects, as the weather was again beginning to be doubtful.

On the rock slopes there were several flowers, and among them I found two dis-

144   *The Karakorams and Kashmir.*

tinct (and, as far as I know, new) varieties of Edelweiss (*Leontopodium Gnaphalium*). Each had a specially characteristic and pleasant scent of its own, while the well-known Swiss variety, that is also very common in other parts of this country, has no distinctive scent.

Our camp was very comfortable ; and, as it had been determined to start early, I set my alarm-watch accordingly, and woke the others at the appointed time. But the weather did not look satisfactory, and so Conway quite rightly determined not to start. However, at 7 a.m. he suddenly decided to do so, and we trudged up the glacier in more or less mist and with occasional small falls of snow. It was a long, gentle snow slope, pretty soft (as, indeed, was only to be expected at that hour of the day) ; then it became steeper for a little, and led up to the top of a pass. There we arrived at 11 a.m., and had a rather animated, not to say heated, discussion as to

Nagyr. 145

the advisability of trying to ascend either of the peaks situated on the two sides of the pass. We were, I think, over 17,000 feet in height.

While we were on the pass the clouds kept shifting a good deal, so that at one time or another we could see most of the view visible from this point. We left there at 12.15, and went back to our camp, where we arrived at 3 p.m. ; it snowed heavily all the afternoon and evening. The next day, Friday (24–6–92), was clear and fine ; but we went down to Sumaiyar, and then came on here to Nagyr, where we found all the others, including Bruce, who has perfectly recovered.

Saturday was a splendid day, which our Ghurkas devoted to playing interminable games of hockey with the native boys. I like these Ghurkas ; they are always exceedingly merry and full of fun, and though but short in stature, are very sturdy and strong. And then everything seems to amuse them.

11

146 *The Karakorams and Kashmir.*

While playing hockey, one of them received an accidental blow, which rather damaged his head; later on he and his companions came to me and drew my attention to the bloody bruise, and laughed over it like anything; they seemed to consider a broken head a most exquisite jest, and the owner of the said head appeared quite proud of it!

Yesterday morning we paid a sort of official-cum-leave-taking-visit to the old Maharajah of Nagyr; his name is Zaper Khan. He is an old and infirm man, who has much difficulty in moving about. He is only nominally the chief, the reigning active one being Secundar Khan, who met us at Tashot. We called on his Highness at about 10 a.m., and stayed there for nearly an hour. His habitation is a very decent one, and has a splendid situation. In the afternoon his Highness was brought to us— he can hardly walk a step by himself—and then there was a "tamasha." ·The royal band put in an appearance, and there was

Nagyr. 147

much dancing, one performer, Ghroda Aman, one of the chief officials (Barra Lumbardar of the place) doing a really good sort of sword dance, which certainly proved that he well understood the handling of a sword. I extracted more information from the Wazir on the subject of the passes. He has now arrived at the point of saying that they were crossed in his youth.

XIV.

HAIGUTTUM, MONDAY, JULY 4.

WE left Nagyr on Monday (27–6–92), at 7.30 a.m., going up the valley, which very soon splits up into several branches, which all join at very nearly the same point, and of which at least three have large glaciers in them, which also unite. The E.S.E. one is the Hispar valley, and the next to this is the Hopar one. Our intended pass, the R Zong La, is up at the head of the Hispar valley ; but the lower end of this is very bad travelling, and to reach its upper part it is better to ascend the Hopar valley for some distance, and then cross into the Hispar valley over a low pass

Haiguttum. 149

in the ridge separating the two. So, accordingly, we went up into the Hopar valley, which contains five principal villages. The first one is called Hakalschal; this we passed, and went on to the second, Rattullu, where we camped. It was a very easy day's march, being well under five miles. The path was very fair, as, in fact, most are hereabouts, in agreeable contrast to those further down; and, as I have already remarked, the people are distinctly much further advanced than those in the lower parts of the valley. On the Monday night Conway informed me that he had decided that, instead of following the plan previously arranged, Bruce and I, with the two Ghurkas, Parbir and Amasing, should separate from the others and cross, *via* the Nushik La (La = pass), a pass in the ridge on the south of the Hispar glacier, leading over into the Basha valley. The further side of this pass has been visited by Englishmen, but so far only natives have crossed it. This is also the case with the

150   *The Karakorams and Kashmir.*

R Zong La, which Conway intends to cross with the others. We are to meet again on the other side of the watershed at Askole. So the four of us left Rattullu on the Tuesday (28–6–92), at 6 a.m. A good path, winding through pleasant fields for rather more than a mile, took us to a queer old dismantled fort at Holshal, which is situated on a low ridge (probably old moraine) on the left bank of the Hopar glacier. Then we crossed this glacier, which is much broken up and moraine covered. There is a very big medial moraine at the junction of this glacier and the Barpu one, and as the path seemed to have a preference for as much moraine as it could find, the walking was very bad till we managed to cross the whole lot and reach the right bank of the Barpu glacier, where a good path once more started on a fairly level stretch of ground between the moraine and the hillside. This space widened and widened till it formed a rather extensive but somewhat marshy "maidan"

Haiguttum. 151

(this seems to be the native name here for any place bearing grass vegetation), called Barfu. From this spot an excellent track went in zigzags up to the ridge that we had to cross to get over into the Hispar valley. It was really a very good path, and, as the elevation of Barfu is nearly 10,000 feet above sea-level, I had a favourable opportunity for carrying out an experiment that I had long wished to make. Some sense, and also much nonsense, has been written on the subject of "mountain-sickness," and the effect of reduced pressure of atmosphere, and various attempts have been made, with more or less (chiefly less) success, to determine the effect of reduced pressure on a man's working efficiency. It is a matter of very great difficulty to obtain sufficiently similar conditions to make the comparison of results obtained of any value. But here it seemed to me that I had a small chance. I have on many occasions determined the maximum rate at which I could go uphill without dis-

152 *The Karakorams and Kashmir.*

tressing myself on a good path, at heights varying from 0 to 8,000 feet above sea-level. I had found that, when in good condition, my rate of ascent had been nearly constant at all elevations inside those limits, and had always amounted to 2,700 to 2,800 feet per hour. Now here was a good path at a considerably greater height, and enough of it; and I certainly was in good condition. So I went up it as fast as I could without distressing myself; by which I mean the fastest pace that I could have kept up continuously without seriously affecting my wind. It took me just twenty-six minutes to the top. I then measured the length of the path and the difference in height with as much accuracy as I could. The length of the path I took was 1,480 yards, and the difference in height 1,220 feet. This gave a rate of ascent of 2,815 feet per hour, and I concluded that, up to a height of 11,000 feet at least, reduced pressure of atmosphere does not apparently affect my working efficiency.

Haiguttum. 153

The way went along near the top of the ridge for nearly a mile, and then descended by steep zigzags into the Hispar valley (which consisted chiefly of scree), to a small green patch of vegetation, where there were a couple of huts. At this spot, which is called Huru, we stopped for lunch, and remained there till a little past 11 a.m. Then we continued our way up the valley. It was rough and desolate in the extreme; scree and rocks there were in abundance; but we only passed one green patch, called Chogmush, on the way up to the village of Hispar. We arrived there just before dusk, after a long and fatiguing day's march. Hispar is a flourishing and highly cultivated place, situated on the left side of the valley, and is rather more than 10,000 feet above sealevel.

There we stopped over Wednesday, the weather being bad. As Hispar is the last inhabited spot up the valley, we had to arrange there for supplies of food and coolies, as it

154 *The Karakorams and Kashmir.*

was bound to take several days before we reached any inhabited place on the other side of the pass we desired to cross.

Just above Hispar, a little over a mile off, the Hispar glacier begins. Our way on Thursday was up along its left bank, mostly on scree, or else on moraine. We crossed three side glaciers, covered with moraine and much broken up, before we reached Makkurum, where we camped, having had nearly eight hours of actual walking. Unfortunately it was not a clear day, and we could not see much. It was a very pleasant situation : there was a small lake, a small maidan, and a few huts inhabited at the time. The next day, Friday (1–7–92), the walking, as before, continued to be abominable. The moraines are much more objectionable than in Switzerland, there is so much of them ; and as for scree, words fail. In the Alps people wax eloquent, not to say forcible, in their language if they encounter a moraine, the passage of which takes an hour

Haiguttum. 155

or so ; here one has them by the day ! The only pleasant spot we passed was a little maidan with a few huts, called Seringshish, charmingly situated in between masses of scree. We crossed two side glaciers, which again appeared to be constructed of seracs covered by moraine matter, and it took us a good five hours to reach our present camp, Haiguttum, the way, as before, being up along the left bank of the Hispar glacier. The weather grew bad on our way up, and on our arrival here it was snowing heavily. This is a desolate spot, about 14,000 feet high, on the left bank of the Haiguttum glacier, some distance up above the junction of the latter with the Hispar. There is some grass and a little vegetation here, and also some brushwood, which makes a rather inferior fuel. When we arrived we found none that was at all dry. We could not get it to burn, so were unable to cook anything. There are about a dozen stone huts here. They are of a kind that I have not seen

156 *The Karakorams and Kashmir.*

before; at the outside they are two-and-a-half feet high. They are built of rough stone, with a little earth on the top; some are long and narrow, in which case their width does not reach 2 feet 6 inches, and others are circular, in which case their diameter is 6 feet in the largest ones, and they are then built dome-shaped. Of course they let wind and weather in through all the interstices between the stones, and are about the worst form of shelter, next to none at all, that I have ever seen. There was no spot on which to pitch our little Mummery tent, the only one we have, and besides that, it would have been but poor shelter under existing circumstances. So we took to one of the long and narrow stone huts, and by spreading the tent and some mackintosh sheeting over the outside we managed to keep comparatively, but only very comparatively, dry inside.

We were short of food; we had some flour and also a little meat, but could not cook.

Haiguttum. 157

Towards the evening it left off snowing, and by 9 p.m., at which time I went to sleep, the sky had partially cleared, and looked (fond delusion!) as if it were going to clear altogether. But on waking at daybreak on the next day, Saturday (2–7–92), I found over four inches of snow had fallen during the night, and it was then snowing very heavily. The clouds were very low down, and we were in the thick of them. So it was quite out of the question for us to start; we anyhow could not do so till we had a clear day to see where the pass was, as we had no idea as to its direction. Another difficulty was the question of food, of which certainly not enough had been brought up. The little meat we had left was raw; we were short of chaputties; we had some flour, but it was quite impossible to get up enough fire to bake or cook. It snowed all that day; in the evening we managed to warm a little Erbswurst soup, which was very soothing. But that was all, and we certainly felt

158 *The Karakorams and Kashmir.*

half-starved. I slept most of the day by way of getting through it, but hunger kept me rather awake in the evening and at night. Later on, at about 1 a.m. (yesterday morning) Bruce woke up and gave me to understand that he felt very, very hollow, and I told him that the principle that nature abhors a vacuum had never before been so forcibly impressed on my mind and stomach. Now I had with me one pound of chocolate, which had been given to me by Conway out of his large stock, and this we had intended to keep sacred for a case of emergency. With absolute unanimity we both came to the conclusion that that time had come. It was still snowing, but I crawled out of the hut and fetched that chocolate, and then didn't we just enjoy it! At daybreak it was still snowing as briskly as ever, and it looked as if it were going to continue to do so for an indefinite length of time. Our food supply was growing more and more deficient, and cooking was still out of the question. So we

Haiguttum. 159

came to the conclusion that Bruce should go back with the coolies to bring up more food, leaving me by myself with what few chaputties there were, so that I should not miss a chance of seeing where the pass was if it cleared up. Accordingly all the others left at 6 a.m., and I looked forward with mixed feelings to a solitary existence of at least three days under conditions which could not exactly be described as the height of cheerfulness. However, on the whole I felt very happy; Bruce I knew to be a determined man, who would not fool about and waste time and opportunity, and I was delighted with having a chance of doing something at last.

About noon it left off snowing, and then it gradually cleared. About 3 p.m. the sun came out for over an hour, and its power was very remarkable. I quite dried my clothes, which was a great comfort. All the snow that had fallen in our neighbourhood disappeared, except in a few sheltered spots.

160 *The Karakorams and Kashmir.*

And at last, much to my delight, I could see where our pass is, just south-west of our camp ; it appears as a well-marked depression in the snow wall on the south side of the Haiguttum glacier. Much to my surprise, about 6 p.m. Bruce and the others returned. They had gone down to Seringshish, where there is plenty of decent wood. There they had converted the remaining flour into chaputties (meat is "off" on our bill of fare), and then, seeing that the weather improved, and that there was a possible chance of the pass to-day after all, Bruce had determined to come back, It was a happy thought. Better do something on half rations or less than spend time and power in walking over exasperating moraines and scree of no interest, in order simply to fill one's stomach more completely. The evening looked very promising, and at night it grew quite clear, and an intense frost set in. We ate some chaputties, and longed for something more substantial. Then we went to sleep more or less, and now we are going to start.

XV.

ARANDU, THURSDAY, JULY 7.

ON Monday (4–7–92) morning the weather was beautiful, and we determined to cross the Nushik La. Our party consisted of Bruce and myself, the two Ghurkas, and Bruce's dog Sapristi. I think I have not yet mentioned that the latter is accompanying us. Since he left Gilgit, Bruce has been accompanied by Wazir Nazar Ali, of Khapulu, who has three Balti boy carriers with him. One of them carries his sword and his umbrella—unusual articles of mountaineering equipment. He is a Balti, and has, at Conway's request,

162 *The Karakorams and Kashmir.*

been ordered by the Kashmiri government to place himself at our disposition. These eight, together with seven men of Hispar, make up our party. As for the seven men of Hispar, we had asked for selected men, who were able to go well on snow, so that they should be good and useful in crossing the pass with us. They have all turned out to be very good plucked and capable men ; I only wish I may have a chance of seeing what they can do under really difficult circumstances. The head man is called Ghulam Ali ; the others are Haider Ali, Khassim Bek, Kujek, Nauros, Shakirin, and Shersi. They are all in the prime of life with the exception of Shersi, who is a very old man indeed. He told me he was eighty years old ; this I can hardly credit, but I certainly think he looks near seventy. The last information I obtained from the Wazir at Nagyr was that the pass had not been crossed for over twenty years. Shersi told me he had frequently been over it in his

Arandu. 163

youth ; at first I looked upon this statement with some doubt, but he clearly showed subsequently that he knew the way well enough. He actually also told me that formerly people used to ride over it on ponies ! This is a statement which, now that I have been over it and know what it is like, I have no hesitation in pronouncing probably legendary.

It is curious to note how, in this country, just as in Switzerland formerly, one hears of passes which were often crossed, and were much easier formerly, but are so no more.

So our party of fifteen started at 4.15 a.m. in beautifully clear weather. The best way goes first along the top of an old moraine, near the end of which Haiguttum is situated. Then the glacier is crossed diagonally to the foot of the snow slope opposite, which is struck at a point considerably to the left of below the pass, the part straight below the pass being too steep and threatened by

164 *The Karakorams and Kashmir.*

avalanches. The whole way up is on steep snow slopes, cut up by many schrunds, and I do not think it is possible to go without traversing some places where at a later hour one might be exposed to falling ice. The slope is of a considerable average steepness. There was one special bit, the steepest we ascended, which was about 150 feet high, being at an angle of $52\frac{1}{2}°$.

As soon as we reached the foot of the snow slope, Bruce, the two Ghurkas and Shersi roped and went together in front, Shersi leading ; then the other followers unroped, and I, by myself, brought up the rear. The most striking object in our procession was the Wazir, with his gorgeous umbrella open ; he also, I presume in honour of the occasion, wore his sword himself instead of having it carried by one of his boys. Sapristi acted like a true mountaineer. When the slope got too steep for him to run about on, he gave up frolicking around, and followed soberly and properly in the steps as they

Arandu. 165

were made. At first the snow was somewhat soft, and for a short piece unpleasantly so, and our progress was regular and uneventful up to rather more than half way up. The place we then reached gave us two alternatives—either to go over a schrund *viâ* a shady snow bridge, followed by a fair snow slope, or avoid the schrund by going to the right. This was very much more the direct way, but involved ascending the steep slope (of $52\frac{1}{2}°$) mentioned above, which consisted of ice covered by a foot of not over-good snow. A slip on this, if unchecked, would certainly have been fatal, as further down, right under this spot, there was an ice precipice. I abstained from saying anything, and asked Bruce to let the natives settle it between themselves, as I was desirous of seeing how far their skill extended, and their subsequent performance proved full of interest. Two of them put down their loads and took off the goat-hair rope they use for carrying. They took a double length of

166   *The Karakorams and Kashmir.*

this, and one tied the doubled rope round his waist in true orthodox style. They then borrowed one of our axes, which so far had not been used. The front man, Haider Ali, who was tied round the waist, started ahead with the axe and cut steps. He was followed by the second man, Khassim Bek, who held the two ends of the doubled rope tied round his stick, which he drove in as he went along. This was certainly much better practice than that usually adopted by Alpine guides. And so they went on till the easier slope above was reached. Then the others followed, and subsequently three of them went back to bring up the two loads that had been left behind. It was really a capital arrangement, and would have done credit to any men. Altogether their performance, and that of the other five, too, was one that not every Swiss guide would care to imitate under similar conditions. None of the loads carried were above thirty pounds, but were all arranged to be inside this limit as far as

Arandu. 167

possible. Just below the top of the pass there was a rather nasty piece of slope with snow that was very rotten. Here our Hispar natives stopped, and said their prayers before proceeding on to it. The top was all corniced, and we did not go over quite the lowest point of the pass, but about fifty feet higher, to the left, where there was the least amount of cornice. Amasing and Parbir cut through it, and I had to bring the rope into use with most members of the party in passing this place. We reached the top of the pass at 9.40 a.m. Roughly speaking, its height is about 16,800 feet, and the view was truly splendid. There were a few small clouds hanging around near the bases of some of the mountains, but not enough to prevent our seeing and clearly distinguishing the giant peaks visible on the north side of the Hispar glacier. Never have I seen mountains that gave such an impression of vastness, while the clearness of the air was something marvellous.

168 *The Karakorams and Kashmir.*

On the map (Indian survey, 27[A] N.E.) three summits are marked—

Snowy peak, 24,108.

Snowy peak, No. 2, 24,593.

Snowy peak, No. 4, 25,503.

As the point at which the top of the pass is supposed to be is not clearly indicated, it is impossible to determine with any considerable degree of accuracy what the prismatic compass bearing of these points, if seen from the top of the Nushik La, should be; but approximately they are 335°, 15°, and 50° respectively. The variation is at present so small as to be negligible in the following considerations. From the top there were actually seven well-marked summits visible, of which the respective bearings were (*a*) 346°, (*b*) 360°, (*c*) 32°, (*d*) 35°, (*e*) 48, (*f*) 64°, and (*g*) 73°. There was no distinct high peak between (*b*) and (*c*). (*f*) was a rock pyramid, and (*g*) a sharper one; in fact, these two might be described as glorified Matterhorns. All these peaks were com-

Arandu. 169

paratively near, and evidently belonged to the mountain system bounding the immediate north of the Hispar glacier, with the exception of (*d*), which was much further off, and which certainly seemed to me *very* much higher than the other summits visible. On the south side there was practically no view; the neighbouring slopes cut it off.

I left the pass at 10.30, the others having gone ahead. For two hours and a quarter our way went over nevé of a gentle slope, which had a few crevasses in its lower parts, necessitating some small *détours*. Then there was about an hour and a half of glacier with the usual ample amount of moraine. We stopped and camped at a grassy spot, called Stiabu Brangsa, by the side of our glacier, which is called the Kero Lungma, at a height of about 13,500 feet.

It had been an intensely hot day; the sun had been shining brightly all the time, and as there was plenty of fresh snow, I rather expected we should have a good deal of

170 *The Karakorams and Kashmir.*

snow blindness. Bruce, the two Ghurkas, and I had worn snow spectacles ; our natives had blacked their eyelids with charcoal before starting. I had a second pair of spectacles (the only other pair with us) ; these I had lent to Shersi ; he wore them part of the time and then passed them on to another man. On our arrival at Stiabu Brangsa, the three Balti boys were foolish enough to wash their eyes in ice-cold water. As a result, which was only to be expected, they all had their eyes rather inflamed, and they suffered somewhat during the two subsequent days. They are a very poor-spirited lot and kept on howling and moaning all the time till their eyes were well again.

Of our seven Hispar men six escaped entirely, their eyes being unaffected, but the seventh man, Haider Ali, was quite blind the next day and had to be led. However, he is a plucky fellow, and did not complain, and has perfectly recovered by now. Our ornamental Wazir, Nazar Ali, was all right ;

no doubt the umbrella, which he had used with a good deal of pride as a sunshade, had helped to protect his eyes.

It froze intensely during the night we spent at Stiabu Brangsa, and the cold, together with our accumulated hunger, woke us up occasionally.

The next day, Tuesday (5–7–92), we left camp at 7.20 a.m., and had several hours of "moraine-hopping" — this most expressive term has been invented by Bruce. On the way down he found a dead ibex near the place where a side glacier, the Orcho Alchori, joins the main one. In a most noble way he presented me with the head, which is a beauty. The horns are a very massive pair, measuring over 42 inches in length, and have a girth of over 10½ inches. The proper way to go on the lower glacier is to keep first along its left-hand bank, and then bear across its end to the right, where the grass path commences when the glacier ends. I had gone a long way in front; misled, however,

172 *The Karakorams and Kashmir.*

by something I had understood the Wazir to say, I kept to the left and went off the glacier, reaching the left bank of the stream issuing. I had a good deal of difficulty in the operations, although I had taken as good a route as there was, and as I thought the others would probably want some assistance in coming down a piece of ice-wall—the last piece before the solid ground was reached—I sat down and awaited their appearance. I mentally cursed the Wazir, as I could see no traces of the good road he had—so I thought—mentioned. I waited and waited, and they did not come, and I began to be anxious. So I went up a little hillock just behind me, and then—well—there they were, trudging along a good path in perfect comfort on the opposite—the right—side of the valley, a path quite invisible from anywhere on the way I had come. I was disgusted, but there was nothing to do except to go across. I tried to cross the glacier stream, which was fairly voluminous and very rapid,

Arandu. 173

by means of the rope method, but several attempts only resulted in my being tumbled head over heels and acquiring sundry bruises. So I at last gave up the attempt and re-ascended the, of course, moraine-covered end of the glacier, and went round. At last I really left that wretched moraine, and got on to the good path at about noon ; my mistake had cost me about an hour and a half of hard work.

The scenery on this side of the range, as far as the valleys are concerned, is entirely different from that on the other. The country has a much greener and richer look, and altogether in character much reminds one of the lower valleys of Switzerland. A little further down the valley we struck a small hamlet called Dambok, where there was some milk, and most refreshing it was, too. The supply was very limited, but what there was disappeared with much rapidity. After four days living on chaputties, and not too much of those, with a mere trifle of other

174 *The Karakorams and Kashmir.*

oddments, one gets up an appetite. Just below this village there is another moraine-covered glacier to cross; it is the end of the Niaro glacier which comes down from the west, and, going right across our valley, butts up against the hillside on the east. I never loved moraines; but I think I am accumulating for them a concentrated hatred bad to beat. However, on this occasion it took only half an hour to cross that piece, and a fairly decent path commenced on the other side. This first skirted the hillside, and then went down to and along the river bank, becoming bad, and in places all but imaginary. After sundry miles of it we arrived at the place where our side valley (which is called the Kero Lungma) joins the main valley (the Basha); the chief glacier of the latter, the Choro Lungma glacier, of course puts its moraine-covered end in the way. It took us an hour and twenty minutes to cross it, and then a few minutes' walk brought us here to the comparatively

Arandu. 175

large and flourishing village of Arandu, which is situated on the right side of the valley, near the end of the glacier, and is about 9,500 feet above sea-level. We arrived at 5 p.m., and our first and most anxious subject for inquiry was the question of food. Here we are at last in a land of plenty. For over two months our food has been chiefly flour and mutton; milk has been scarce, eggs and chickens nearly unknown, and butter absent, except on rare occasions; and as for the last four or five days we had been on half allowance, and that of poor quality, we are in good condition to appreciate the good things here. We accordingly had, on our arrival, far more appetite than we knew what to do with. The evening that we arrived, we, *i.e.*, Bruce and I, had two chickens fried in butter, a dozen fried eggs, half a dozen large chaputties fried in butter, and half a gallon of milk. We were really too tired to eat what, in the circumstances, would have been a square meal, and we slept like tops when we turned in.

176 *The Karakorams and Kashmir.*

We woke up at 6 a.m. yesterday morning; we could have slept a lot more, but it seemed to us that breakfast was a much more important consideration. So we breakfasted. We had three quarts of milk, a dozen fried eggs, and ten fried chops, besides chaputties fried as usual. Then we thought we should do till lunch, which we decided to have at noon. I have remarked that in this expedition I had noticed with regret a practice of breaking plans which had been made. On this occasion I am sorry to say Bruce and I fell into it. For that breakfast did not seem to last long. I had another quart of milk at 9 a.m. to keep me going; and at 10 a.m. we concluded that the time for lunch had more than come, and so we had some on a modest scale. It consisted of nineteen fried eggs and chaputties. After lunch Bruce went to sleep for about three hours and a half, and I passed the time in writing, repairing garments, and consuming another quart of milk.

Arandu. 177

When Bruce woke up we had some tea, and later on, dinner. This we had intended to be on a modest scale, and to consist merely of a chicken and a few chops. When we had finished these, we found that Parbir had fried us ten eggs as well. However, our appetites were in such a healthy state that it was distinctly a comfort to us that he had done so. Then we had some milk, and finally turned in. This morning we are going to leave here; we have just paid our account for our party. The items and prices paid are as follows :—

				Rs.	Ans.
8 seers [1] milk @ 1 anna ...	...	...	...	0	8
53 eggs @ 6 for 1 anna ...	...	...	...	0	9
2 sheep @ 2 rupees 8 annas	...	...	...	5	0
1 sheep @ 3 rupees	...	...	...	3	0
16 seers wheat flour	...	...	...	1	0
20 seers barley flour	...	...	...	1	0
5 seers butter ...	...	...	...	1	12
3 chickens @ 4 annas ...	...	...	...	0	12
				R.13	9

[1] One seer by weight is a little over 2 lbs.; by measure, about 1 quart.

178   *The Karakorams and Kashmir.*

Then we distributed various small sums as " bakhshish " for bringing word, etc., so that our total expenditure came to exactly 14 rupees.

XVI.

Skardu, Wednesday, July 13.

WE left Arandu on Thursday (7–7–92) at 7.20 a.m., and continued our way down the right-hand side of the valley. The way was occasionally a fairly decent path along pleasant hill slopes, but part of it was along the river bed, where it was sandy and very heavy walking. It was a tremendously hot day, and several pleasant-looking camping-places seemed to invite us to stop and rest. More particularly did we look with longing eyes on a charming village called Kingero Don. But we sternly marched on, and were very pleased when we reached the village of Doko

180   *The Karakorams and Kashmir.*

at 1.45 p.m., where we had arranged to camp. This village commands a fine view of Gangchen, and also of Shalchakbar, the mountain next south of it, two imposing peaks rising on the opposite east side of the valley. The green partly-wooded slopes in the immediate vicinity cut off the view to the west. The houses of this village are built in the same style as those of Arandu; they are different from those on the other side that we have come from. Many of them have two storeys. The lower floor, which has thick stone and mud walls, is built somewhat into the ground. On this a roof of wood and earth is made; and as of course all the ground is on a slope, one cannot at first sight say whether one is walking on the roof of a house or on solid ground. Then in most cases on this roof a second floor is put, the sides and roof of it being of wattles. The house is thus suitable for all extremes of temperature, and of course the extremes are great here.

Skardu. 181

As Doko is about 9,000 feet above sea-level, it must become very cold in winter, whereas at the time of our visit it was quite tropical.

The next day we marched down the valley, and passing the villages of Tsibirri, Nyesole and Hemasil, went as far as Chutrun, which is well over 8,000 feet above sea-level. This village is celebrated for its hot spring, which is of considerable volume. There are several very convenient bath basins built. In one of them we enjoyed a good bath and had all our things washed. The water is absolutely clear and, to judge by its taste, or rather want of it, is practically pure. What its temperature may be where it leaves the earth I could not ascertain, as that place was enclosed and not accessible to us; at the entrance to our bath basin it was 39° C. Like the day before, we had a hot day; particularly so in the afternoon. At 2 p.m. it was 34° C.; 5 p.m., 31°; 6 p.m., 29½°; 7.15 p.m., 26°.

182   *The Karakorams and Kashmir.*

The minimum in the night was 23°, at 4 a.m., and that with an absolutely clear sky. We both felt rather uncomfortable and oppressed during the night and slept very little ; it was indeed a contrast to our nights while near the Nushik La. At Chutrun they call to prayers for daybreak with drums and pipes, making a noise which, I should think, would move even the most hardened sinner. Anyhow it moved me— though not to prayers—and I started from Chutrun at 5.10 a.m. (temperature 25°) to do our last march, for the time being, to Molto, while it was still comparatively cool, leaving Bruce to enjoy another hour or two of sleep before he followed. We knew that there would be some delay at Molto while arrangements were being made for us. As I went down the valley it became much cooler, and at 7.15 I reached Molto, a flourishing village. (At 8 a.m. the temperature was 21° C.) Hereabouts the Basha valley, along which we came down from

Skardu. 183

Arandu, joins the Braldu one, some way up which is the village of Askole, to which we intend to go later on. The two together form the Shigar valley. I gave the necessary orders touching the preparation of a raft, which was the method of locomotion we intended to adopt from this place, and then ordered lunch to be prepared, so that it might be ready when Bruce arrived. To pass the time, I discussed things in general with the head man of the village, and found that the names given on the map are different from those in use at this place. He called the valley we had come down " Brasha," not " Basha." " Ligup " he called " Lagap "; " Matuntoro " should be " Matunsoro." " Dishupagon " he called " Poishupar "; and the mountain on the other side of the Shigar river, marked "Busper," he called " Bachmu." I gradually began to feel very hungry, and as Bruce did not appear, I at length ordered up lunch. My appetite was still in such a good condition that I not only

184   *The Karakorams and Kashmir.*

ate up what I had intended for myself, but also what I had meant for Bruce ; and then, very thoughtfully, ordered the same total amount—a dozen eggs, and extras—to be prepared for Bruce.   I thought he also might have a similar appetite.   He turned up just when this second lunch was ready ; he had felt very hungry on the road and had stopped for lunch on the way.   However, as this second lunch was ready, he thought he might as well have some again, and so did I ; and we finished it with much satisfaction. We rested till 2 p.m., and then, being informed the raft was ready, we proceeded down to the river.   Our destination was really Askole, up the Braldu valley, but we had to go on to Skardu, the nearest trading centre, situated some way further down near the junction of the Shigar and Indus rivers. For Conway was much in want of various supplies, such as rice, dried apricots, salt, pepper, sugar, and also, more particularly, small change.   Money is a frightful nuisance

Skardu. 185

here. No change can be obtained anywhere except in the large towns, so one has to carry the bulk of one's money in small change, which . is weighty and cumbersome. Our goat-skin raft, on which we then embarked, was a queer craft; it consisted of twenty-four inflated goat- and sheep-skins tied under a sort of rough wattle. The entire skins had been removed from the animals without cutting; the openings were closed by being tied up with a strip of birch-bark, the ends of which were merely joined by an overhand draw-knot. I rather wondered that this knot resisted at all; however, birch-bark strips evidently have peculiar properties in the way of knotting, as the knots stood fairly well, and did not often give way. The skins leaked a good deal, so that it was frequently necessary to blow them out again. Our crew consisted of four men, armed with long poles, which were used as punt-poles, boathooks, and even as paddles. It was certainly a very secure craft, and

186 *The Karakorams and Kashmir.*

could not possibly upset in any rapid ; but for dampness it was inimitable. The Shigar river, down which we went, is a succession of rapids ; these gave us a good deal of amusement and wetting at the same time. Several times we ran into shallows, and had to get out and walk till we reached deeper water. Our boat was, roughly speaking, in the shape of a square ; it revolved more or less continuously, so that one could readily without trouble admire the whole view. Our rate of progress must occasionally have been very great. We stopped, after just one hour's run, at Kaiyu, a village on the right bank of the river. This is over five miles, measured in a straight line, and is of course a good deal more allowing for bends. There we camped ; and the next morning we again embarked on our gallant craft. About three hours' run took us to a landing-place on the left bank of the river, from which we walked up to Shigar, a village, in fact almost a town, on the slopes above

Skardu. 187

our landing-place. Here we had luxury indeed — green peas, potatoes, and any amount of ripe apricots. How many of the latter we ate I do not know; that may be left to the imagination. As my stock of tobacco was exhausted, I was delighted to find that that article, which is not so much a luxury as almost a necessity, was procurable here, and I smoked native tobacco with much enjoyment. It had rather a curious but not at all unpleasant flavour, due to the admixture of a little Indian hemp; but this I did not mind at all—in fact, I very soon began to consider it an improvement.

On Monday we went down with the raft as before, and in about an hour and three-quarters reached the junction of the Shigar and Indus rivers. Here we landed, and walked up along the right bank of the Indus, one of our crew easily carrying our ship on his back. Then we embarked again to cross, which took just twelve minutes. We arrived, of course, much

188 *The Karakorams and Kashmir.*

further down on the opposite side, owing to the force of the current. Then we walked up along the left bank of the river to Skardu, meeting on the way the local Rajah, who, with the usual motley array of followers, came to salute us. Here, at Skardu, our first visit was to the post-office, which was in charge of a very intelligent native called Maulavi Ramazán Ali, and there we found a large accumulation of letters. Then we went on to the solitary Englishman stationed here in charge of some native troops, Captain Townshend, who received us most kindly, and entertained us during our stay here. He was very pleased at our arrival ; it was some time since he had seen a white man. He was out of whisky and grieved thereat ; he explained to us his supplies had somehow managed to be delayed or lost, and that he was short of everything in consequence. But a couple of hours after we turned up his missing coolies did so too, with the supplies

Skardu. 189

intact, and among them there was a case— a precious case—of whisky. So he determined that we should have a "tamasha" of our own that evening, to which noble resolution we of course gave our unanimous consent. It was a great "tamasha." Townshend played the banjo, and sang very comic songs. Bruce and I are not of much use in the singing line; but in the drinking department we were "all there," and strictly stuck to business. Yesterday we spent a quiet day; in the afternoon I went to the polo ground, where I was much amused by seeing some of the native soldiers playing football under Townshend's supervision. He introduced it among them, and they evidently enjoyed it very much.

This morning another Englishman, D. W. Churcher, an old schoolfellow of Bruce, arrived. He is on a shooting trip, and hearing that good Shapooh were to be found up this way, he decided to go with us to Askole, and then up to Punmah, where he expected to find good sport.

XVII.

ASKOLE, TUESDAY, AUGUST 2.

ON Wednesday (13-7-92) Bruce and I
left Skardu for Shigar at 4.30 p.m.
on two of the smallest ponies I have ever
seen. There is a biggish ferryboat here,
which took us over the Indus. My pony
was not of much use, so I got off and walked
most of the way, while Bruce went ahead
merrily. It soon grew pitch dark, and as I
had no lantern it was not easy to see and
find the road, of which, of course, I knew
nothing, so I did not reach Shigar till 10
p.m. A decent pony would have taken me
over in two hours, and if I ever go to
Skardu again I shall have a pleasant inter-

Askole. 191

view with the Kotwalli (native official) for not supplying me with a decent animal.

The next day (14–7–92) we waited at Shigar for Churcher. He arrived from Skardu at about noon, and in the afternoon we rode off to Skoro. This time we had very good ponies, and galloped nearly all the way. It is really remarkable what rough ground these ponies will gallop over.

We camped at Skoro, and the next morning (15–7–92) started up the side valley called the Skoro Lumba to cross the Skoro La (La = pass) to Askole.

The way is up a narrow valley, which in some places might almost be called a gorge. We left Skoro at 6.25 a.m., and arrived at our camping-place, Kutza, at 1.30 p.m. There is a big hut there at a height of rather over 12,000 feet. All around it there was Edelweiss in profusion. It was absolutely identical with the Swiss (scentless) variety, and this was the first place at which I saw any of this kind.

192   *The Karakorams and Kashmir.*

We left our camp the next day (16–7–92) at 5.30 a.m.   At first we had about 2,600 feet of ascent of the usual description, a rough and occasionally invisible path up grass and rocky slopes.   The next 2,000 feet to the pass gave me some amusement, involving a bit of climbing and the cutting of several steps.   Amasing was carrying my ice axe, and had walked off with it, and so I had to go back to the habits of our remote ancestors of the stone age ; in other words, I cut sundry steps in the ice with a sharp triangular piece of stone.   It took me three hours and three-quarters, excluding halts, to go from Kutza to the top of the pass. There is hardly any view, for the hills in the immediate neighbourhood cut it off.   The descent from the pass was down a gentle snow slope, followed by glacier and the inevitable moraine, of which, on this occasion, we, however, only had three-quarters of an hour, and then down the grassy and fertile valley.

Askole.   193

At 5 p.m. we reached a convenient place to camp, about 13,600 feet high, and there we stopped for the night. Our coolies were very much done up, and were very late in arriving ; the last ones did not turn up till the next morning. The next day, Sunday (17–7–92), we came on here to Askole. Leaving our camp at 7 a.m. we went down in three-quarters of an hour to the flourishing village of Thla Brok. Never before have I seen such quantities of Edelweiss ; patches of a square yard and upward in size absolutely covered with it were scattered all over the hillside. Then, bearing rather to the left, we went to the village of Monjong, which is situated in the main Braldu valley on the left bank, just opposite to Askole. From there half an hour of good path, winding chiefly between rich fields, took us down to the Braldu river, which we had to cross on our way here. The former rope-bridge had been carried away last year, and when the natives heard that we were coming they

194   *The Karakorams and Kashmir.*

set to work to rebuild it for our benefit. It was not quite finished when we arrived, and so we had to wait a little. After crossing it, the path here to Askole took us twenty minutes.

This is a flourishing village about 10,400 feet above sea-level; we have a very pleasant camping-ground, a green spot with plenty of trees. Supplies are plentiful; there are chickens, butter, eggs, milk, sheep, and flour in abundance. We thought it was just possible that Conway and his party, coming over the R Zong La, might have arrived here before us; but nothing had been seen or heard of them on our arrival. So, on the Monday, Bruce left to go up the Biafo glacier to see how this side of the pass looks; he came back on Tuesday, and reported that the pass appears to be easy on this side. Then he, together with Churcher, went off on Wednesday to do some shooting, and stopped away about four days. He took the little tent with him, and so, in view

Askole. 195

of possible rain, I intended to take up my quarters in the verandah outside the mosque. But the natives objected, and installed me instead in a very comfortable house. During these days it was mostly fine weather, but, unfortunately, Conway had specially asked me not to do any of the several expeditions I could have made at this time, as he did not want anything of importance done in his absence; so I had to be content to wait till he arrived. He had told me that he expected to arrive here by the 15th of July, but taking into consideration that he had two inexperienced men with him, I certainly thought he would take longer than that, if indeed they persevered on their road.

On Thursday (21–7–92) Zurbriggen arrived in the afternoon and brought news. After Bruce and I had left the others at Hopar, he, with Conway, had attempted the ascent of a mountain up the Shallihuru glacier. But his boots had given out, and consequently he had been unable to proceed.

196   *The Karakorams and Kashmir.*

It took Zurbriggen a long time to relieve his feelings on this subject ; he uttered the most blood-curdling threats against the bootmaker (a Swiss one) who had made them.   He also was strong in his abuse of the (qualified) "imbécile" who had prevented him from taking his spare pair of boots with him. So they had rejoined McCormick and Roudebush, and then made their way, *viâ* Hispar, to near Haiguttum.   Then he had taken Roudebush and a party of coolies over the Nushik La by a different route, a more difficult one than that taken by Bruce and myself.   He had had great difficulties in compelling the coolies to go the more difficult way.   They (not unnaturally) had strongly objected to this proceeding.   Then he, after leaving Roudebush, who had gone on to Skardu, had returned over the Nushik La to Conway and McCormick.   With them and natives he had come over the R Zong La.   On this side, when some way down the Biafo glacier, he had gone ahead, leaving

Askole. 197

Conway to photograph and McCormick to sketch, and come on leisurely.

He told me the pass was a long one, but otherwise quite easy. The men from Hispar evidently knew the way over, and were acquainted with the best camping places not only on the other side, but also on this. He would undertake to drive a hundred head of cattle over it in a week from Askole to Hispar, and troops could readily cross it. Bruce returned on July the 23rd ; during the next two days coolies from Hispar dropped in at intervals, and finally, on the 26th, Conway and McCormick arrived here. Conway gave me a description of their pass, but it differed much from the one I had from Zurbriggen. According to Conway, the pass was certainly not practicable for troops or cattle ; the Hispar men knew nothing of the way, and he did not believe the pass had ever been used by the Hunza and Nagyr people for raiding. Be that as it may, I cannot decide the question ; but there are fortifications up

198 *The Karakorams and Kashmir.*

above Askole to defend any approach from the side of the Biafo glacier which I have examined. One fort is marked on the Indian survey map, and I presume they were put up for use, not for ornament.

On Wednesday (27–7–92) we had a sort of general meeting, at which it was arranged that I should leave the expedition. There had been a good deal of friction from time to time, and, as we had now been some two and a half months in the mountains without making a single ascent of importance, having only crossed two previously known passes, I was not anxious to go on, and accordingly we agreed to separate. Conway and the others left here on Sunday (31–7–92) in order to go up the Baltoro glacier and try something there.

In the absence of any appliances or supplies, it is of course out of the question for me to attempt any big climbing, and so I intend to travel along leisurely and at my ease. I had a very affecting farewell parting

Askole. 199

from our Hispar men ; may it be my good fortune some day to meet them and travel with them again!

Yesterday (Monday, 1–8–92) I saw an exceedingly fine solar halo, far and away the finest I have ever seen. When I first noticed it, about one-sixth of the circle was cut off from view by the hillside. There was only an extremely thin film of cloud in the sky, not visible except on very careful inspection. There must have been some special condition of the air. At 10 a.m. the halo was finest ; the entire circle, showing the colours plainly, was clearly visible ; it then gradually faded away, till at 11 a.m., it had quite disappeared. In the evening the moon showed a faint but well-marked halo, which lasted for certainly two hours ; for how much longer I do not know, as I went to sleep. There are any number of exceedingly good boulders hereabouts, and I spent much time not only in climbing them myself, but also in setting natives to climb them. I

200 *The Karakorams and Kashmir.*

arranged regular rock-climbing competitions among them, my object being to see how these natives compare with Swiss guides. I was more than surprised at the feats performed, and arrived at the following conclusions (which apply to natives of this Askole district only, as compared with the good rock-climbers among Alpine guides, both being considered from the boulder-climbing point of view).

The *best* man I found would beat the best guide I have ever seen with the greatest ease over any kinds of rocks.

For "Platten" (smooth slabs) most natives would beat the best Swiss.

For climbing depending on small holds, the average native would be beaten by the average guide ; but the difference is not great.

As for "friction - climbing" (rounded smooth rocks), there is not much to choose. The *best* native I found was not altogether an exceptional man here, as several ran him very close. I take rock-

Askole. 201

climbing here simply from the gymnastic standpoint. Their judgment of rocks was not good; in fact it was singularly bad, considering the quality of their performance. It is great fun starting the native at this sort of thing : the promise of the smallest copper coin of the country (a Kashmiri pie, equal to one-eighth anna) as prize is enough to set the whole village off trying rocks.

I have engaged some natives as attendants ; the head man is from Poljo, a village further down the valley. Strange to say, he understands a few words of English. He informs me that further down the valley there are much better climbers, and that if I will give large prizes he will send on word and have all the good climbers assembled for a display. I told him that I would go to the expenditure of even a whole rupee for prizes, if there were really good men ; and I told him to send on word that I would stop a day at Biano and there hold such a competition.

XVIII.

SKARDU, FRIDAY, AUGUST 12.

I LEFT Askole on Tuesday (2–8–92), and, instead of recrossing the Skoro La, went down the valley. For some two hours I went along a good path on its right side, mostly through rich cultivation, till I arrived at the flourishing village of Chongo, where I made a prolonged stop. The natives here were very sociable, and what struck me particularly was that the girls and women came and squatted around too, and looked at me with much interest. In all the places to which I had previously been in these mountain districts I seldom saw any representative of the female sex, and then only more or less

Skardu. 203

by accident, as they disappeared at once in evident dismay at being seen by a stranger. But here it was quite different, and the men also were much more friendly than any I had previously seen. So I produced some tobacco, and we smoked a hubblebub (a native pipe, of the chibouque pattern with the smoke passing through water) together and discussed things. There was one very geographical old native present, who drew me a plan of the upper valley. He told me he had been over both Mustagh passes, and from his description it seems to me that the proper name for K2 is Skinmang, or Dapsang. But as I had no map with me it was impossible to absolutely verify the fact. The Biafo glacier he described as the " robber road," which seems to support my belief in the truth of Zurbriggen's account of the R Zong La.

From Chongo the way went down to the river, which I crossed by a rope-bridge, and then continued along the left bank, till I reached the small village of Pakora, where I

204 *The Karakorams and Kashmir.*

stopped to camp. Womankind here wears a curious sort of dress, decorated sometimes with brass chain and oddments, and in some cases with rough sapphires and really fine work. I tried to buy one of the latter sort ; but the results were alarming. The owner was a rather pretty girl ; and it must be remembered that here, as at other times, we could only converse by roundabout methods. It was settled, however, that I was to pay eighty rupees, and that the article purchased should be delivered in the morning ; a proceeding which seemed to me quite reasonable, as the girl was wearing the dress at the time of purchase.

In the morning, however, the dress did not turn up, but the girl, clad in an ordinary dress, did ; and it appeared that what I had purchased was not the dress, but the contents. I explained that I had no use for them, and they then gave vent to what I am quite sure was something very superior in the way of heathen profanity. I made a

Skardu. 205

mental note to the effect that the women in this village, as opposed to those whom I had previously met in the district, are forward persons. So I departed from the village at 5.20 a.m., and just below it crossed to the right bank of the Braldu river by a rope-bridge. This was in a beautiful spot ; just under it there were rapids which were almost falls. The noise of the water was nearly deafening, and while crossing I was enveloped in a cloud of spray ; seldom have I been in a more impressive place. The path then continued along the right bank of the river, and soon became very rudimentary indeed. At 7 a.m. there was a most disagreeable side stream to cross. Not that there was much water in it, but it had abominably soft and sticky mud banks ; I had to take off my footgear and wade through greasy, filthy mud up to my knees. Then the path vanished altogether, the hillside consisting of a mixture of consolidated mud and stones. Occasionally it was very

206 *The Karakorams and Kashmir.*

steep, and at one place we had to cut over thirty steps. Later on, a little past 8 a.m., we reached the banks of a very steep side nala ; an exceedingly curious place, such as I have never seen or heard of before. In shape and formation it was simply a deep nala, with almost perpendicular sides of the usual character ; no water came down it, but at intervals avalanches of filthy-looking black, wet mud, a most horrible and disgusting sight. The upper part was not visible, but a big cloud of dust hung over it, showing that somewhere on the hillside continual stone falls took place. It was not a nice place to cross, and we waited some time before attempting it. First of all steps had to be cut down our side of the nala. In forty-five minutes I counted thirty-one mud avalanches ; then it became brisker, and thirteen came down in the next ten ; then hey slackened a bit, and we crossed. One man went up to a place which commanded a view for some way up, and gave the word

Skardu. 207

when it was safe to go. Wading through the mud in the bottom of it was not pleasant, nor was the ascent of the lower portion of the opposite bank, which was also mud. Going up through soft deep snow is not nice, but it isn't a patch on mud.

It took to past 10 a.m. before we were all over. Just on this side of the nala there is a tiny warm spring, in which I cleaned myself with much comfort. Then an hour and three-quarters of very rough walking took me to the very pleasant village of Rhomboro, which is situated at the spot where an important side valley, the Hoh, joins the main one. At the head of this valley there is also a native pass, the Braldu La, leading over to the Hispar glacier. Here I stopped for lunch and waited till it was cooler, and then walked in a little over an hour to the village of Biano, where I stopped to camp. On arrival I found a large crowd of natives expecting me ; men had come from far and wide in order to show their climbing

208   *The Karakorams and Kashmir.*

powers and gain unheard-of wealth ; no doubt many had also come to gaze upon the strange, very strange white sahib who took an interest in such things. I certainly believe I am the first man of the sort that they have come across.

On Thursday I stopped at Biano and held my great competitions. With regard to rock-climbing, my general conclusions at Askole, namely, the good quality of the natives, were confirmed, and, if anything, strengthened. The best man here was somewhat superior to the best man there, and all round I also had a better average. I tried to test their tree-climbing qualifications, but without success. The most difficult tree I could find was only twenty feet from the ground to where it branched off ; for the first five feet above ground the bark was rough, the other fifteen were smooth ; diameter, five feet above ground, equal to eleven inches. This could, of course, be readily ascended without any special difficulty. The

Skardu. 209

champion rock-climber was called Ghulam Ali, and he was presented with the large sum of one rupee. I daresay he never before possessed such vast wealth, and when I presented sundry smaller sums to other competitors enthusiasm rose high. I addressed a little speech in English to the meeting, of which of course they did not understand a word, and they cried "Shabash" (Bravo!) Then I distributed tobacco, and we smoked native pipes together; in fact, we had a high old time. Here, for the first time in India, I had two mosquito bites. There were only very few mosquitoes, and I only saw one, which I killed when it bit me on my ankle. I also was bitten on my left wrist, but I did not see the beast. The bites swell up tremendously, but are not at all irritating compared to those of other insects. There is one insect in this valley which I have not seen, and I do not know, except through its bite; but that insect, to judge by its biting power, seems descended

210 *The Karakorams and Kashmir.*

from a crocodile, and by its venom from a rattlesnake.

I left Biano on Friday last (5–6–92) at 4.45 a.m., and continued my way down the valley to Pahar, a very small hamlet, where I arrived at 6 p.m. The path there was very bad, continual uphill and down, and I was very satisfied when I reached camp. The entire food supplies of the place, apart from corn, consisted of three eggs, which I promptly finished. I fondly hoped that the hens of the place would behave in a reasonable way, and produce more eggs by the morning. Alas! my hopes were disappointed, and so Saturday's breakfast was rather a mockery. I started at 6 a.m., feeling that this was indeed a hollow world, and that I was a sample of it. We saw any number of rabbits, and also the tracks of two bears, a large and a small one, which had been made the same morning. Alas for the absence of a shooting tool! Not far down is the junction of the two valleys, forming

Skardu. 211

the Shigar one, and when we reached Tandero I demolished eggs in plenty, and then had a nap. Here I procured a very decent pony ; but a saddle was a luxury the place did not run to, and so I did without. The rate of the pony-hire was eight annas per day, which does not seem extravagant.

That pony was an amusing little beast ; it had a strong liking for epicycloid curves, rapidly performed. I think it even went in for chortoids, but of this I am not certain ; my attention was not fixed on considering the subject from the purely mathematical point of view. However, ultimately I persuaded my steed that a straight line had geometrical merits, and arrived at a village called Kashumal, which is the usual stopping place. I did not like the look of it at all ; the inhabitants were the most wretched I have yet seen. There were any number of goîtres, cripples, sores, etc., and I was told the water was very bad. So I rode on to Tsildi, a pleasant and healthy-looking village,

212 The Karakorams and Kashmir.

where I camped. The next morning (Sunday, 7–8–92) the natives of the place produced with much pride a curious and antique saddle, which they proceeded to put on the back of my pony. It was an imposing structure, and raised my seat at least eight inches. I mounted with a good many misgivings, and found that I had to balance myself very carefully, as when I gave the least sideway movement the saddle did likewise. The stirrup-leathers, which by the way were made of goat-hair rope, were much given to breaking, and ultimately repeated knottings so shortened them that I gave up their use altogether. Just before reaching Skoro, a heavy rain shower stopped me for more than two hours; and then I rode on to Shigar, where I arrived at noon, and stopped till Tuesday morning.

In this neighbourhood a species of soft soap-stone, green to yellow and grey in colour, is found. This is readily cut by steel tools, and is accordingly made into a variety

Skardu. 213

of articles, such as cups, lamps, pipes, etc. The pipes are of two patterns ; either simple pipe heads to use on a hubblebub of the usual Oriental pattern, or short pipes, like the ordinary English ones. A good deal of the stone is also exported in the rough.

On Tuesday I rode on here to Skardu, crossing the Indus by the ferry boat. My first visit was to the post and telegraph office, where I found a large accumulation of letters and papers for me. The head official in charge, Maulavi Ramazán Ali, was most courteous and polite, and has done everything he could for me during my stay here, acting occasionally, in cases of difficulty, as interpreter. He is evidently a superior man ; when I was going to bestow bakhshish on him he refused to accept any, and said that if I want to do him a great favour I am to send him an English book when I arrive home, as he is very fond of reading English books and he is unable to

214   *The Karakorams and Kashmir.*

obtain them. I have accordingly promised to send him one.[1]

My excellent natives, who have accompanied me here from Askole, decline to go

---

[1] Nearly two years later I sent him two books ("Robinson Crusoe" and "Charles O'Malley") from London. I subsequently received the following characteristic letter from him :—

"RESPECTED SIR,

"I most humbly and respectively beg to state that I have received your present : two books, which you favourably and kindly bestowed me. I was always remembering you and was thinking perhaps you might have forgotten me to fulfil my request and was very anxious for it, but it was also going on in my mind that the gentlemen like you are not dispromising their trust,

"my respectful sir I am well, and trust you are well with your royal family—and am very much thankful for your so much rememberance.

"May God give you health of life and prosperity in your long age.

"please inform me if you can favour this humble man by your any service or order—and lead for any good occupation of livelihood avoiding the servantness of Indian difficulties,

"Yours obediently,
"MAULAVI RAMAZAN ALI,
"Telegraph master."

Skardu. 215

on any further, as their crops want attending to. As it is, they have already come further than they originally agreed to—namely Shigar, and they have left with much apparent sorrow. But I really believe that they were actually sorry. I have engaged some fresh men, of whom the chief is Mahamet Dju, a queer little man who wears a continual smile, and certainly does know how to cook. There is plenty of food here; eggs, butter, milk, flour, chickens and sheep give plenty of variety. In the vegetable kingdom there were green peas, potatoes, rice, and any amount of apricots and mulberries. My food, so far as these luxuries go, costs me six annas a day, and I live on the fat of the land. Tobacco, tea, and pepper are also procurable. I have, but without success, tried to obtain a tent; the small Mummery tent, which is the only one that I have, is of very little use here, as it cannot stand a strong wind or rainfall; and excellent as it is for the purpose for which it was designed,

216 *The Karakorams and Kashmir.*

namely for a high mountain bivouac, it is quite useless for ordinary travelling purposes if the weather is bad.

To-day I start for Srinagar.

XIX.

SRINAGAR, MONDAY, AUGUST 29.

I LEFT Skardu on Friday (12–8–92) on a pony. This animal much resembled the coolie of these parts, in that it went at a great rate for a very short way, and then stopped dead, generally very suddenly, which was somewhat discomposing. Then he wanted considerable persuasion to start again, unless I waited till what he considered a proper interval had elapsed, and then he went off just as suddenly. The way was up a steep rocky valley, the Burye, which in places almost was more like a gorge than anything else. It rained a good deal during the afternoon ; and we stopped for the night

218　*The Karakorams and Kashmir.*

at a spot where there was wood and water, and otherwise nothing particular to distinguish it. It rained heavily during the night; in the morning it cleared up somewhat, and so I started at 7 a.m. At its upper end the valley enlarges and forms a sort of little plateau, surrounded by a rocky ridge, arranged horseshoe fashion. This little plateau is quite 15,000 feet high; and the pass in the ridge which we crossed, called the Burye La, is about 15,700 feet. There was a little snow-field just at the top of the pass, and it was not in good condition; so I had to dismount and lead the pony over. Just as I reached the top it began to sleet; and for the rest of the way we had a variety of hail-sleet-rain. At 2.30 p.m. I reached a brangsa called Buchmemat. Here are some stone huts of the same build as those at Haiguttum, but larger, some of those of the long pattern being four feet wide. But these also were very far from weatherproof. From the Burye pass the way is

Srinagar. 219

(to the next pass) over a very undulating plateau, the Deosai plateau, which is about 12,000 to 14,000 feet high, and quite un-inhabited.

The next day, Sunday (14–8–92), we stopped at Buchmemat, as the weather was awful. The following day, Monday, was just as bad ; but we had only taken one day's extra food with us (there are no habitations between Skardu and Mapanun, and of course no food is obtainable), so it was no good stopping where we were, and we made a start at 7 a.m., and went on till 12.30 p.m. in a most furious rain. Then we found an overhanging rock, which offered some small amount of shelter, and we were also fortunate enough to find some wood so that we could do some cooking. In the afternoon the rain turned to snow, which at first melted and later on lay. At 6 p.m. a remarkable change for a short time took place. By that time there were quite two inches of snow on the ground, and it was

220 *The Karakorams and Kashmir.*

freezing. Then the snowfall slackened, and it suddenly changed to a very warm drizzle; it felt quite muggy, and by 6.30 not a trace of snow was left. Later on, however, it snowed again. After midnight it cleared, and then froze intensely. Next morning it was clear, and the snow-covered plateau looked very fine at sunrise; but we only had a few minutes of sun, as it clouded over almost at once.

We started at 6.15 a.m. It rained and snowed a little, but not much, at odd times during the day. We had four fair-sized rivers to ford this day; but as we had been pretty wet for some time that did not add much to our inconvenience. We camped by a river called Marko Chu; here there are a few stone huts of the same pattern as usual. We arrived there a little after 2 p.m. In the afternoon it rained a little, but in the evening it cleared up, and the night was very cold. It froze intensely, and all our things, which had not had an opportunity

Srinagar. 221

of drying since the day we crossed the Burye La, were stiff. My coolies suffered a good deal, and seemed to be a good deal more affected by the cold and wet than I was. Anyhow, I do not recommend anybody to cross the Deosai plateau in bad weather, unless he is provided with a decent tent.

Fortunately the next morning (Wednesday) was fine and cloudless. Very grateful to us was the rising sun, and thanks to the power of its rays, which is of course considerable at such an elevation, we managed to dry ourselves and our things.

The pony also had managed to arrange matters to his satisfaction. He had evidently not approved of our actions, and had come to the conclusion that he did not care to continue in that sort of way. During the night at Marko Chu he broke loose and went off, and in the morning nothing was visible of him but his tracks, which led back in the direction of Skardu. So I had to

222 The Karakorams and Kashmir.

proceed on foot, and what with getting dry, and examining pony tracks, we did not start till nearly 9 a.m. This day I saw a good many "drin," apparently a kind of marmot. These were the only signs of life that I saw on the plateau. They were reddish-brown little animals, who seemed to know that I had no firearms, and derided me accordingly. I also saw a fair number of bees. In the afternoon we crossed a small pass, where the plateau terminates. Just on the very top of the pass is a fair-sized lake, which drains both ways; but chiefly towards the side from which I came. When it gets drier, it would only drain in that direction. Then the path descends considerably, and at 5 p.m. we reached our camp Chota Duce, a few of the usual stone huts. There was a sharp frost in the night. The next morning (Thursday, 18–8–92) an hour's walk took me to the top of another small pass; and coming down from this the Dorikun pass road is joined.

On my way down to the Burzil storehouse,

Srinagar. 223

I met an Englishman, who, I gathered, was a doctor in the service ; and shortly afterwards I met an English officer and his wife, who were travelling Skardu-wards. I know not their name ; but she appeared to me like a vision of celestial beauty and grace. For the first time since untold months, I saw a white, feminine face—the face of a charming English girl. But I do wonder what they thought of me! Taking me all round, I think it would be difficult to imagine a more ragged - looking, disreputable object. My supply of soap had given out at Skardu ; and as none had been procurable there I had to content myself with plain water, which is not a very efficient cleansing agent when used by itself. My garments had been new once—in the long, long ago—and had been patched in sundry places with sheep-skin. Stockings I had none ; and my footgear consisted of an old pair of tennis-shoes also patched with sheep-skin.

However, nevertheless we exchanged very

224   *The Karakorams and Kashmir.*

pleasant greetings, and they told me many items of interesting news.

The whole place was very different indeed from what it had been in April. Then there was snow almost everywhere, and where the ground was visible there were but few traces of vegetation on it. Now the valley was just one rich mass of green, with grasses, etc., up to four and five feet high. By the Burzil storehouse there was a big encampment, in charge of a native hospital assistant, who received me most hospitably and gave me some milk. A heavy transport of stores for Gilgit was going on, and the road had been and was being improved very much ; new bridges were being and had been built. I went on to Mapanun, meeting train after train of loaded mules and ponies on the way. The next day (Friday, 19–8–92) I went on to Gurez. At this place I was met and received with much effusion by the Tesseldar, who seemed exceedingly pleased to see me again. He is really a fine-looking man, and

Srinagar. 225

looks more a gentleman than any other Kashmiri that I have seen. I have unfortunately some reliable acquaintance with bronchitis; and through this circumstance and my drugs I had been able on my previous visit to cure him of bronchitis. His gratitude had lasted since then. He now came to me with a lot of money, which he wanted me to accept. He said I had been a long time on the journey, and by now no doubt was short of money. So he had brought me some which he begged me to accept, adding that, if I wished to return it, I could send it to him at any time, or else repay him at my next visit. This date was too near to that of the Greek Kalends for me to be able to accept the offer; but it was gracefully and kindly made. I stopped there for several days, and was much entertained by the Tesseldar. Of course, conversational powers were somewhat limited, as he did not understand Hindustani very well (nor did I for the matter of that) and I know no

226 *The Karakorams and Kashmir.*

Kashmiri. However, we made up for want of language by plenty of tobacco, and were very sociable. I left on Friday last, and from there I came back *via* Kanzalwan and Tragbal Chok. There also the road had been much improved, and of course there was no snow. The top of the pass was, however, enveloped in shifting mists on the Kashmir side for a considerable distance. On Saturday, on the way down to Bandipur from the pass, I met Gofara, who had been one of our boatmen at our previous visit. He had heard I was coming that day—how, goodness only knows, and so came to meet me, bringing me some grapes, some lovely peaches, and some bread. I think the bread was the greatest luxury of all. Chaputties are all very well, but they do get mono-tonous.

At Bandipur I went on board Gofara's boat, which I have hired for the time, and thought I should be at peace, but the mos-quitoes thought otherwise. They came, not

Srinagar. 227

singly, not by tens or hundreds; no, it seemed to me as if by hundreds of millions were nearer the mark. So I wrapped myself up in blankets and tied handkerchiefs round my face and my hands, and baffled the enemy to some small extent; but nevertheless the next day my face was beauteous to behold. I doubt whether my nearest relatives would have recognised me. There was, however, one great comfort; although the bites swell up tremendously, very little irritation is produced.

Then I came by boat here; on my way up through the town I stopped at the house of Samad Shah, a well-known native banker who has a general sort of shop, and purchased a mosquito-curtain and also a decent suit of clothes, and have pitched my camp at the Chenar Bagh; and here I propose to stop some time.

XX.

SRINAGAR—CONCLUSION.

SOON after my arrival at Srinagar I once more had a bad attack of diarrhœa, but it soon yielded under the kind and skilful treatment of Dr. Deane, whom I shall always remember with feelings of the liveliest gratitude.

I stopped at Srinagar for rather more than two months, and I had plenty of amusement during the time. On most days I was buying things all day long, from morning to evening. That sounds as if I had been purchasing vast quantities, and giving up all my time to this primitive commerce. This, however, does not follow. If one wants to

Srinagar. 229

buy a thing in those parts, it is a slow, a very slow process, unless, indeed, one is foolishly desirous of paying n times the value. n varies from $1\frac{1}{2}$ to 50 ; the average seems to be about 4 to 5, but this depends on the article and the purchaser. So that if one is desirous of buying things at a reasonable rate, it is necessary to bargain with the native in the way that he is accustomed to.

Thus I bought an old Yarkand jug. It was brought to me one day, and the whole of that day was devoted by its owner to the negotiations, and also the whole of the following day ; on the third day the purchase was arranged, and the heathen was joyful. In the meantime I had gone on with my ordinary avocations ; writing, eating, and doing whatever I had to do. While I was so engaged, the merchant squatted down with my servants and smoked and discussed things ; and as soon as I was disengaged he was ready to begin bargaining again.

The heathen is very fond of leaving the

230 *The Karakorams and Kashmir.*

ultimate decision of the price to be paid to chance. Thus when, after a long course of bargaining, the price I was prepared to give was not far off that which he was ready to accept, he generally suggested that we should toss, and thus decide which price it was to be.

The most remarkable instance I had was in the case of a Yarkand knife, with a jade handle and a rather ornamental sheath. This was brought to me the day after I arrived at Srinagar, and the owner began by asking 200 rupees for it. He came to bargain with me about it at least every other day, and it was not till the day on which I left Srinagar that we finally tossed whether I should give 5 or 7 rupees for it. I regret to say that he won the toss. On most occasions I was singularly lucky, and the natives said that I had the best " kismat " that they had ever known.

The only things that seemed to have a fairly definite value were copper work and

Srinagar. 231

silver work; but with them of course the quality differed, and of the silver (which is supposed to be standard silver) a good deal would not stand analysis. I had a complete blowpipe set with me, by the help of which I examined things that appeared doubtful; and the knowledge I so acquired, when displayed to the natives, struck them often with amazement, as they were quite ignorant of any such methods of analysis.

Precious stones were also subject to a sort of mineral metempsychosis. Thus cairngorm was passed off as topaz; white topaz and sapphire as diamond; many different things as jade; while, in addition to native stones, cat's-eyes, rubies and sapphires of apparently Paris manufacture were also common. The first stone merchant who called on me gave me the benefit of these conventions, and looked displeased at my remarks. He finally succeeded in riling me, and I gave him two minutes to remove himself in; he had a lot of things strewed

232 The Karakorams and Kashmir.

around on the floor of my boat, so I thought it fair to allow him a little time. He remained a short time over the two minutes, and then I relieved him of the necessity of removing himself. In this way it became known in the land that I understood stones ; and the heathens thereafter who came to try and sell stones to me, only named stones that there was no earthly doubt about.

Ultimately the native dealers came to the conclusion that I was a very great authority on stones indeed; and in a good many cases, where two stone dealers had quarrelled between themselves as to the quality or nature of stones which had passed between them in some transaction or other, they mutually agreed to appoint me as arbitrator, and my decisions were accepted without question.

I had a great deal of amusement in one way and another with these men. On one occasion a dealer was trying to sell me stones, and in looking over his stock I

Srinagar. 233

noticed a little packet which he had not undone. When I asked him what he had there, he said that the parcel contained beautiful stones, but not for sale to me ; and, opening it, he displayed some exceptionally fine specimens of cut sapphires as they are made in Paris.

Now there was in Srinagar at this time a young American. It appears to be the practice in that great country, to which he belongs, for nature to select a certain number of the population as scape-goats, crowding in upon them all the habits of swagger, insolence, and conceit for which the average population has no use. Such scape-goats are then sent out into the wilderness, whether Europe or elsewhere is immaterial, so that it be outside America ; and this particular American stranger then in Srinagar was one of them. I had happened to see him for the first time when he was dealing with a stone-dealer, and I had ventured to warn him that he was about to buy doubtful silicates as

234 *The Karakorams and Kashmir.*

precious stones; but he had attributed my caution to British swagger, which would not recognise in a foreigner the true critical judgment of stones.

So I told my stone merchant that I thought this American sahib would buy the " stones."

" Go, therefore," said I, " and offer them to him ; do not tell him that they are what they are not, but tell the sahib that he is a wise sahib, and can judge for himself, and then he will buy." " What price shall I ask him, 50 or 60 rupees ? " said he. " Not so," I answered, " ask him for 2,000 rupees, and bargain with him at great length, or he will not buy ; and certainly do not take less than 500 rupees."

So he went off, and I forgot about the transaction, till some days afterwards I became aware of a heathen who was addressing me in the fullest Oriental metaphor, describing me as his father and his mother, the protector of the poor, the sun round

Srinagar. 235

which his miserable universe revolved, and so on, and I saw it was the stone merchant. He had offered the "stones" to the American sahib for 2,000 rupees. The counter proposal was 100 rupees, at which the soul of the jeweller had rejoiced, for even that price would have left him a good profit. But he had held out, and ultimately had obtained 800 rupees from the white man, who in exchange received some of the best pieces of Paris-made coloured glass that I have come across, and is probably displaying them at the present time to such of his acquaintance as do not understand stones. But the stone merchant was not satisfied with telling me of his conquest; he proposed that, this wealth having come to him solely from the suggestion of the Heaven-born (by which he meant me), I should take half of it for my share. I explained to him that I was not in Kashmir to make money, and that if I had helped him I was glad enough, and that I could not take his money. But I pointed out to him that there was another world as well as this, and that he should make thanks' offering for the goodness of Allah in sending him such an American sahib. "Go, therefore," I said, "and give those 400 rupees to a holy man, and ask him to say prayers for the souls of myself and you." This, he subsequently assured me, he had done; and if the American sahib ever happens to see this account, perhaps he will accept my present acknowledgment of the spiritual service for which I am indirectly indebted to him.

The city of Srinagar is in one respect a very curious one: there is no wheeled traffic in it whatever. It would be quite impossible to have any except in one or two places; the majority of the streets are much too narrow.

I wandered a great deal about the city; I went to all sorts of workshops and looked at the processes of manufacture and at the

Srinagar. 237

tools used. The latter are very primitive, but handled with great skill and infinite patience, so that really good work can and does result. But that is only so in comparatively few cases; cheap and inferior work is largely manufactured and sold to the white man who comes here, and who, at least in most cases, knows nothing of workmanship, and whose execrable taste is rapidly undermining the true artistic feeling which seems to be the natural gift of almost every native.

Very interesting indeed were (much to the surprise of some Englishmen there, who could not understand how I could not see anything in " those wretched heathens ") the natives to me. I spent many hours with them, smoking native tobacco in the native fashion, and discussing all sorts of things with them ; and I may say that, taking them all round, I have never met men of another race to whom I have taken such a liking.

238 *The Karakorams and Kashmir.*

In the early part of October Conway arrived, and gave me news of what they had done since I had left them at Askole. They had attempted the ascent of one of the larger peaks up the Baltoro glacier, but luck had been against them, and they had only succeeded in reaching a minor point on one of its ridges.

One day I was invited by my silversmith to dinner. It was a gorgeous meal ; all the dishes, etc., that were used were of gold and of silver, and I felt like a prince in " The Thousand and One Nights." The dinner was very good, but what it was composed of was, in most instances, a matter of some doubt to me. This was the menu :—

Pulao (rice, roast meat, and spices).
Mutejan.
Pul.
Zokowangwen.
Kabab (small pieces of roast meat, highly flavoured).

Srinagar. 239

Goshtab (a soup of strange taste).
Mit.
Shom.
Gawgidj.

The drink was tea; first of all there was Chinese tea of very fine flavour, prepared in the way that we are accustomed to, and after dinner there was "Kashmiri" tea, which is made by infusing a mixture of tea and sundry flavouring herbs, and adding butter and salt to the liquor so obtained. It sounds a curious combination, and the first taste of it seemed horrible to me. The second taste was not so bad, and by the time that I had finished the first cup I liked it so much that I had several more, and during the remainder of my stay I had it after every meal.

Occasionally I moved about a little; I camped at various different places round the Dal lake, which is near Srinagar. And so ultimately came, much to my regret, the

240 *The Karakorams and Kashmir.*

time when I had to leave. I had some imperative engagements in the South of India, and if it had not been for these, perhaps I might have been there still—who knows?

THE END

APPENDIX.

ROUTES.

SRINAGAR TO BANDIPUR.

ABOUT 35 miles by road; counted as two marches. It is usually done by boat ; by water the distance is about 37 miles.

BANDIPUR TO GUREZ.

About 35 miles ; counted as four marches. The Rajdiangán Pass, 11,950 feet high, has to be crossed : in winter it sometimes becomes impassable for ordinary travellers. My net walking time was $14\frac{1}{2}$ hours.

GUREZ TO ASTOR.

There are two alternative routes. Bruce and Zur-briggen took the one *viâ* the Kamri Pass (13,260 feet high) ; about 77 miles, counted as seven marches. The others and I went by the Dorikun Pass (13,500 feet high) ; about 82 miles, counted as eight marches. My net walking time was $32\frac{1}{2}$ hours.

These routes are not practicable during winter to

242 *Appendix.*

ordinary travellers, nor to loaded coolies. But there are few days on which a passage could not be forced by good men.

ASTOR TO BUNJI.

About 48½ miles ; counted as five marches. My net walking time was 20 hours.

BUNJI TO GILGIT.

About 37 miles ; counted as four marches. It would take about 14 hours' walking *at my usual pace.*

Thus the whole distance from Srinagar to Gilgit was nearly 240 miles. Since then, improvements in the road have resulted in saving some distance, so that it may now be taken at about 230 miles.

THE BAGROT VALLEY.

From Gilgit to Dewar is rather over 5 miles. From Dewar to our camp at Dirran was about 7 hours' walking ; from the latter to our Gargo camp took me 5½ hours, the last 2½ hours being over moraine-covered glacier.

On the way back I took 1½ hours in descending this glacier, and from its end to Gilgit my net walking time was 13 hours.

THE MANUGA VALLEY.

Dewar to Barhet, 3 hours 50 minutes.
Barhet to Bure, 45 minutes.
Bure to Derbana, 55 minutes.
Derbana to Surgen, 1 hour 10 minutes.

Appendix. 243

In the reverse direction :—

Surgen to Derbana, 1 hour.
Derbana to Bure, 30 minutes.
Bure to Barhet, 45 minutes.
Barhet to Dewar, 3 hours 35 minutes.

GILGIT TO GULMAT.

Gilgit to Nomal, 6 hours 20 minutes.
Nomal to Chalt, 6 hours 30 minutes.
Chalt to Gulmat, 3 hours 30 minutes.

GULMAT TO TASHOT.

Just beyond the fields of Gulmat there is a deep nala. From this nala the path winds for 1,260 yards through cultivated ground. Then there are 880 yards of rough path, fairly level, through barren ground, followed by 70 yards of steepish ascent. Here there is a large cairn ; 1,490 yards further is a bridge, crossing a stream issuing from a glacier, the end of which is about a mile off ; 280 yards beyond this bridge is the village of Pisan, with a fort a little on one side of the road ; 1,240 yards on is a bridge over another glacier stream, and 440 yards beyond it the fields surrounding the village of Minappon begin, and the path winds through them for 1,350 yards. Then the path is rough and through barren ground ; it descends from the hillside, and for some distance is near the bank of the river. On the slopes above it are, however, two flourishing villages, Mia-char and Dadiwan. Two miles forty yards from Minappon the path divides into two branches at the entrance of a side nala. (The valley up this nala is called the Peker valley.) The left-hand branch of

244 *Appendix.*

the path goes on to a bridge over the Hunza river, which it crosses. It is the main road to Baltit, the capital of Hunza. The right-hand branch of the path goes up the side of the nala in zigzags—a steep ascent of 650 yards—and then a level 100 yards further on is the camping-ground at Tashot.

The total distance, from camp to camp, is rather over 7 miles ; net walking time, 3 hours.

Tashot to Nagyr.

The path goes up steep zigzags for 800 yards ; it then turns into the lower end of a nala, which gradually widens out till it becomes open ground ; 1 mile 80 yards from the top of the zigzag is the corner of the fort of Pakkar ; the path goes along its wall on the right side of it ; 130 yards on is its entrance, facing a polo-ground, and opposite is an old mosque. The path continues through fields for 920 yards ; then down steep zigzags over rough ground for 80 yards, and then the fields of Hakutshar begin. It goes along these fields for 860 yards, when it reaches the village; the fort, with several old watch-towers, being further down the slope. Further on the cultivation becomes sparser, and the last piece is passed 770 yards further on. Then the path is very rough, going along a sand and scree slope for 1 mile 200 yards, till the fields of Shaiyar begin ; 600 yards on is the polo-ground, the village and fort being further down on the left ; 1,040 yards on is a small hamlet, the name of which I could not discover ; 700 yards on is the village of Askurdas. The path continues along the slope for 1 mile 660 yards ; then it goes down into a big nala for 540 yards, when

Appendix. 245

it comes to a good bridge. On the further side of this bridge a steep ascent of 190 yards leads to the village of Sumaiyar. From this village rich cultivation continues for 1,150 yards; then it becomes poorer and poorer, and 1 mile 400 yards further on it becomes quite barren. At this spot there is an old watch-tower just on the left of the path.

The path then goes along a rocky slope for 1,220 yards; here there is just a patch of cultivation, which looks more like a garden than anything else; 1,200 yards on cultivation begins again regularly; after 1,660 yards of it (broken only by one small sterile nala), the corner of the fortified town of Nagyr is reached. From this to our camping-ground (situated by the polo-ground) was 480 yards.

The total distance, from camp to camp, is a little over $11\frac{3}{4}$ miles; net walking time, 4 hours 45 minutes.

Nagyr to Baltit.

The path leading to Sumaiyar is first taken for a short distance; then the path to Baltit diverges to the right, and traverses down till the Nagyr river is reached. Here there is a rope-bridge, and on its further side the way is round and over the projecting spur of rock—very rough walking—till another rope-bridge, over the Hunza river, is reached. After crossing this there is a steep ascent to the camping-ground, which is situated a little below the village and castle of Baltit.

Net walking time, 2 hours 30 minutes.

Daranshi Pass.

From Sumaiyar the path ascends first along the right bank of the Sumaiyar river for 15 minutes;

246 *Appendix.*

then it crosses a bridge and keeps along the left bank for 4 hours, when the end of the glacier is reached. Our camp was about 15 minutes higher up. From this point we followed the moraine for 2 hours, till it merged into the snow; then bore to the left for two hours, till we reached our camp, on the névé under the rocks on the south side of the western ridge of the Daranshi peak. From this we ascended, going nearly due east, over gentle snow slopes, the last piece being a little steeper, in 3 hours to the top of the pass.

The descent from the top of the pass to our highest camp took 2 hours 30 minutes; and from there to Sumaiyar 4 hours 15 minutes.

Nagyr to Rattullu.

The path winds through cultivated fields for 2 miles, when a village called Torl is reached. There the path divides; the lower one goes mainly along the bottom of the valley, and is wider and better for horses and mules than the upper one, which is, however, distinctly shorter and better for pedestrians. The upper path skirts the hillside, following sundry watercourses in succession, and passes by the village of Hakalshal to the village of Rattullu, by which was our camp.

The total distance by the upper path, from camp to camp, is 4 miles 1,490 yards; net walking time 2 hours.

Rattullu to Hispar.

The path winds through fields, reaching the village of Holshal in 1 mile. It then ascends a little, reaching in 440 yards the old dismantled fort of Holshal,

Appendix. 247

which is situated on the top of the old lateral moraine on the left bank of the Hopar glacier ; 440 yards of rough walking bring one to the edge of the glacier. This is much broken up, and being covered with moraine *débris* is very bad walking. We went straight across it ; it took 21 minutes to the middle moraine, dividing the glacier from the Barpu glacier. At first the path ascends a little, and then for some distance goes along fairly level in the direction down the glacier ; it then ascends straight to the top of the moraine ; this point is reached 20 minutes after leaving the glacier proper. This part of the moraine is old and solid ; then the path descends to new moraine, now in course of formation, and crosses the Barpu glacier, here also covered with moraine *débris ;* this takes 18 minutes. Then the path goes along for 16 minutes between the hillside and the moraine to Barfu ; and then zigzags in 26 minutes up to the top of the ridge which separates the Barpu valley from the Hispar one. The path then goes to the left along the face of this ridge, but descending, at first gradually, and then more rapidly ; in 1 hour Huru is reached, which is about 1,800 feet lower than the top of the ridge at the point where it is crossed. From here a steep descent of 10 minutes takes one to near the level of the stream ; and then the path, which is very rough, goes along it for 46 minutes, often going up and down over pieces of rock, till a bridge is reached by which one crosses to the right bank of the river. Keeping up along this, Chogmush is reached in 1 hour 17 minutes ; and 1 hour 26 minutes beyond this a side stream is crossed. Here are some fortifications, and this side stream is occasionally a very awkward obstacle. Five minutes beyond it is a

248 *Appendix.*

bridge by which the main river is crossed to its left bank ; and after a steep ascent of 10 minutes the fields of Hispar begin. Fifty minutes on through these —in the course of which a deep nala with a stream, the Bulapat nala, is crossed—was our camping-ground.

Nearly all the way up the valley to Hispar is over rock and scree. Net walking time, camp to camp, 8 hours.

HISPAR TO HAIGUTTUM.

The path goes up the valley, keeping fairly level, for 45 minutes from Hispar. Then it divides into two branches. The one to the left goes on to the glacier, and crosses it to its right bank, where there are several grazing grounds. The right branch continues for 10 minutes, and then takes to the moraine-covered Hispar glacier, going along it for 15 minutes. Then it leaves it, going up the slope to the right, and then along it ; for 45 minutes all is scree, and the path, which so far is well-marked, becomes practically invisible. Then the slope becomes less abrupt, with a good deal of wild vegetation on it, and 30 minutes on a nala, with a fair-sized stream in it, is crossed. On the further side of it is an overhanging piece of rock, very convenient for one or two people to camp under, a purpose for which it is occasionally used. Thirty minutes on is a small "maidan" with two huts, and 10 minutes beyond it the Toramuk glacier, a side glacier coming from the south, is reached. This is moraine covered, and takes 30 minutes to cross. The path (which here again is visible) then skirts along the slope, reaching in 45 minutes another side glacier, also moraine covered, which takes 1 hour 15

Appendix. 249

minutes to cross. This is followed by rough and bad walking for 30 minutes along the slope ; then the way goes on to the main glacier, also moraine covered, and goes up close along its south bank for 1 hour. Then another side glacier joins in, also moraine-covered, which takes 30 minutes to cross. Five minutes beyond this is Makkurum, where there is a "maidan" and a few huts ; 30 minutes on is another side glacier, also moraine covered, which takes 30 minutes to cross. Then the path (which is here faintly visible) goes a little way along the side moraine of the main glacier ; it then turns to the right and makes a steep ascent, through shrub, to the top of an old grass-covered moraine, which is reached in 15 minutes. Between this and the hillside is "maidan" ; 20 minutes on are a few houses, Seringshish ; 30 minutes on there is another side glacier, also moraine covered, which takes 45 minutes to cross. Then the path goes for 45 minutes along the moraine of the main glacier ; then it traverses a grassy slope, keeping fairly level, for 30 minutes. It then gradually ascends, bearing round the corner to the right, reaching the camping-ground, where there are some small rough huts, in 1 hour.

Net walking time, camp to camp, 12 hours 45 minutes.

HAIGUTTUM TO ARANDU.

The way goes first along the top of the old moraine on the right bank of the Haiguttum glacier, and then down to the glacier, which is reached in 10 minutes from the camp. The glacier is then crossed diagonally in 30 minutes to the foot of the opposite slope, rather to the left of the part situated straight under the

250 *Appendix.*

pass. The snow slope is then ascended, bearing somewhat to the right, till the pass is reached in 4 hours 30 minutes. The descent is over gentle slopes of névé for 2 hours 15 minutes ; then there is a medial moraine which is crossed towards the left in 15 minutes. Then, still bearing to the left, there are 15 minutes of glacier, followed by 15 minutes of its left lateral moraine. Then an old grass-covered moraine is followed for 45 minutes, to Stiabu Brangsa, which is a grassy spot in a corner where a glacier joins the Kero Lungma, the main glacier. This side glacier is crossed in 45 minutes ; then the path goes along the grassy slope on the left bank of the main glacier for 1 hour, when the spot is reached where the Orcho Alchori joins the main one. Then, bearing diagonally down across the latter to the right —here all moraine covered—for 1 hour, its end is reached. A good path from here goes along the right side of the valley ; in 50 minutes the small village of Dambok is reached ; then the moraine covered end of the Niaro glacier is crossed in 30 minutes. Further on the path, which keeps to the right side of the valley, is bad ; in 1 hour a place with a few rough huts, called Alibeki Brangsa, is reached, and 40 minutes on is the moraine-covered end of the Chogo Lungma glacier. This is crossed in 1 hour 20 minutes to its lower, right end ; then after 10 minutes of good path the camping-ground is reached.

Net walking time, 16 hours 10 minutes.

ARANDU TO SKARDU.

Arandu to Doko, 4 hours 50 minutes.
Doko to Chutrun, 2 hours 40 minutes.

Appendix. 251

Chutrun to Molto, 2 hours 5 minutes.

Molto to bank of river, 30 minutes.

Then by raft to the junction of the Indus and Shigar rivers, to the right bank of the Indus, 4 hours 55 minutes ; then walk 35 minutes along the bank ; cross by raft to the left bank in 12 minutes, and walk to camping-ground in 1 hour.

SKARDU TO SKORO.

Skardu to Shigar, 2 hours by pony.

Shigar to Skoro, 1 hour 10 minutes by pony.

The Indus river has to be crossed between Skardu and Shigar. There was a large, well-appointed ferry-boat.

SKORO TO ASKOLE BY THE SKORO LA.

Cross the Skoro river to its left bank ; at first the path goes along the river, and then along the slope a little above it. In 1 hour 40 minutes Chuchen Brangsa, a minute village, is reached. Forty minutes on the valley divides ; the path, which is fairly well marked, goes up the left branch, frequently crossing and recrossing the river, but keeping near it, for 1 hour 20 minutes. Then it leaves the river, and ascends the slope to the left in a series of steep zigzags for 40 minutes. Here it divides ; the left-hand branch reaching in 20 minutes Kuehechan Brangsa, which consists of a few huts. The right-hand branch bears along the slope, rising gently, for 30 minutes, when the camping-ground, Kutza, is reached. From here the path strikes straight up the slope to the pass, which is reached in 3 hours 45 minutes from Kutza. On the other side of the

252 *Appendix.*

pass a gentle slope of névé leads down for 30 minutes, followed by 45 minutes of moraine-covered glacier. Then the way, descending the valley, is at first over rough stone, and then grass, merging gradually into a fair path. In 2 hours 10 minutes the village of Thla Brok is reached. The path next traverses to the left, going round a projecting hump, and then descends steeply diagonally to the left, in 1 hour 20 minutes to the village of Monjong. From here the path winds through green fields down to the river, which is reached in 30 minutes and crossed by a rope-bridge. The ascent to the village of Askole takes 20 minutes.

Askole to Skoro by the Valley.

From Askole to Chongo, along the right side of the valley, takes 2 hours 10 minutes. Below this a rope-bridge is crossed to the left bank of the river, and Pakora is reached in 1 hour. Just below this a rope-bridge is crossed to the right bank ; in 1 hour 40 minutes a nala, with much mud, is reached. Then the path becomes exceedingly bad ; in 1 hour 10 minutes a side nala is reached, down which avalanches of mud come, and which sometimes is very troublesome to cross ; 1 hour 45 minutes on is Rhomboro, and 1 hour 10 minutes beyond it is Biano. Just below this a rope-bridge is crossed to the left bank ; in 1 hour Poljo is reached ; 50 minutes on is Geu Ongo : 2 hours 5 minutes on is Blokpe Blok ; 3 hours 25 minutes on is Pahar ; 3 hours 15 minutes on is Tandero. From here I rode, on a pony, through Yeno, Kashumal, and Tsildi to Skoro in 4 hours.

Appendix. 253

Skardu to Gurez.

About 88 miles ; counted as 8 marches. Three passes, the Burye La (15,697 feet), the Sarsingar (13,860 feet), and the Stakpi La (12,900 feet) have to be crossed. Most of the way, which is a good pony track, is at a height of over 12,000 feet, and consequently is difficult to traverse except in the height of summer.

The Gresham Press,
UNWIN BROTHERS,
WOKING AND LONDON.

14 DAY USE
RETURN TO DESK FROM WHICH BORROWED

LOAN DEPT.

This book is due on the last date stamped below, or
on the date to which renewed.
Renewed books are subject to immediate recall.

AUG 2   1962

LD 21A–50m-3,'62
(C7097s10)476B

General Library
University of California
Berkeley

20/-3

ImTheStory.com

Personalized Classic Books in many genre's

Unique gift for kids, partners, friends, colleagues

Customize:

- Character Names
- Upload your own front/back cover images (optional)
- Inscribe a personal message/dedication on the inside page (optional)

Customize many titles Including
- Alice in Wonderland
- Romeo and Juliet
- The Wizard of Oz
- A Christmas Carol
- Dracula
- Dr. Jekyll & Mr. Hyde
- And more...

Lightning Source UK Ltd.
Milton Keynes UK
UKOW06f0020290716

279503UK00016B/505/P